SMALL GROUP
MINISTRY
VOLUNTEER HANDBOOK

SMALL GROUP
MINISTRY
VOLUNTEER HANDBOOK

Equipping You to Serve

Scripture quotations are taken from the Holy Bible, New International Version. Copyright © 1973, 1978, 1984, 2011 by Biblica, Inc.® Used by permission. All rights reserved worldwide.

First Edition: Year 2021
Small Group Ministry Volunteer Handbook / Outreach, Inc.
Paperback ISBN: 978-1-951304-66-9
eBook ISBN: 978-1-951304-67-6

CHURCHLEADERS
PRESS

Colorado Springs

SMALL GROUP
MINISTRY
VOLUNTEER HANDBOOK

Equipping You to Serve

Written by
Mikal Keefer

General Editor
Matt Lockhart

CHURCHLEADERS
PRESS

Colorado Springs

CONTENTS

INTRODUCTION

to the *Outreach Ministry Guides* Series

Each of you should use whatever gift you have received to serve others, as faithful stewards of God's grace in its various forms
(1 Peter 4:10).

*T*his handbook is part of a series designed to equip and empower church volunteers for effective ministry. If you're reading this, chances are you're a church volunteer. Thanks for your willingness to serve!

Several things make this handbook unique:

- The content is specific and practical for your given area of ministry.
- The information is compiled from experienced ministry practitioners—folks who've worked, served, and helped to train others in this particular area.
- It's written with you—a ministry volunteer—in mind.

Within these pages you'll find three sections. The first gives a brief overview of fundamental principles to provide you with a solid foundation for the ministry area in which you're serving.

Section 2 unpacks various skills related to the responsibilities involved. Understanding what is required and assessing if it's a good fit is helpful in creating a ministry team that is effective and serves together well.

Finally, Section 3 provides a multitude of practical ministry tools. These ideas and tips will help you demonstrate Jesus' love to the people you serve.

Whether you're a first-time volunteer or a seasoned veteran, my prayer is that the information and practical tools in this handbook will encourage and assist you. May God bless and guide you in your ministry!

— **Matt Lockhart,** General Editor

INTRODUCTION

to the Small Group Ministry Volunteer Handbook

A confession, right up front: were I forced to choose between attending a church service or meeting with my small group, I'd choose my small group.

Every time.

Yes, gathering with my entire church family is important. It's vital to show up to pray, praise, serve, give, to hear God's word proclaimed, and to share testimony of God's faithfulness. But if I had to choose, I'd still rather open the Bible with my small group in Dave's living room. Or hike with my group along that stream running behind Tom and Emily's farm. Or spend Saturday morning at Nancy's house helping her haul soggy furniture out of her flooded basement.

Small groups are where life and faith intersect. You find space and time to talk about fears and to deal with doubt. They're a safe place to celebrate success and mourn loss with people who know your story. They're the friends you can call when you've got a sleeper sofa to get up three flights of stairs. Small groups are where you can talk about the Bible without having to pretend you've already figured everything out.

The friends I've made in small groups have sustained me through dark times and prayed me through hard decisions. They've held me up when I struggled to stand on my own and given me opportunities to support others. They've reflected the love of Christ when I had a hard time seeing it on my own.

I know small groups can change lives because they've changed mine. As you put the tips and training you'll find in these pages into action, you'll see lives change, too.

You'll discover how to build your small group on a solid foundation. You'll hear from small group veterans about how to lead groups, what to do when things don't go as planned, and how to avoid common leadership land mines.

There are strategies for taking your group deeper, and how-to insights for leading prayer, empowering service, and building lasting, Jesus-centered relationships. This isn't just theory—these are solid suggestions from people who've been where you're going. Think of this book as your pocket-sized coach as you dive into leading your small group.

And those lives you'll see changed?

One of them will be your own.

— **Mikal Keefer,** Author

SECTION 1

THE WHAT AND WHY OF SMALL GROUPS

CHAPTER 1

WHAT THE BIBLE SAYS ABOUT SMALL GROUPS

*n*ot much, actually.

While there are some solid biblical examples—Jesus and the twelve, the early church fellowshipping together in their homes (Acts 2:42-47), and Paul meeting outside the city gate by the river with a group of women gathered for prayer (Acts 16:13)—there's not an explicit directive to go forth and form small groups.

So, why small groups? If the Bible doesn't specifically call for them, why should your church promote them? And why should you bother leading one?

Here are four biblically-based reasons for small groups—and any one of them is reason enough for your church to embrace small group ministry, and for you to open your heart and home to one.

Small groups are a practical way to "one another"

Smaller gatherings provide the opportunity to do something the Bible instructs us to do: for believers to "one another." That is, to connect in supportive, caring ways. Here's a sampling of how that's to look (with a more complete list in Chapter 21):

- Tolerate and forgive one another (Colossians 3:13)
- Serve one another (Galatians 5:13)
- Bear one another's burdens (Galatians 6:2)
- Pray for one another (James 5:16)
- Be hospitable to one another (1 Peter 4:9)

- Speak truth to one another (Ephesians 4:25)
- Encourage and build one another up (1 Thessalonians 5:11)

Notice these "one anothers" happen best in the context of relationship. Most worship services aren't ideal places for relationships to form. A brief "passing of the peace" or smile across the sanctuary doesn't really help believers bear each other's burdens, hold one another accountable, or pray together.

Small groups let us enter into and be present in one another's lives. They give us a place to be faithful to our "one another" calling.

Small groups can break through barriers

Research confirms what you already know: we tend to form friendships with people who are similar to us in terms of age, education, race, and attitudes.[1] This means in a world desperately needing to embrace diversity, we're wired to gravitate to people like . . . us. Small groups are a place your church can encourage people who aren't alike to connect—and connect deeply.

When Brad attended a financial skills class at his church, he got more than budgeting help. "At the first meeting we wandered in and took seats at round tables," he says. "I'm in my 20's so I found a few people in that age range and sat with them."

But then the organizers shuffled attendees around. "I ended up at a table with a couple in their 60's and with people of different backgrounds that I'd not met before," says Brad. "At our table we had a lawyer, a mechanic, a couple people struggling to find work—it was a diverse group."

---

1   *Birds of a Feather Do Flock Together*, Wu Youyou, David Stillwell, H. Andrew Schwartz, Michal Kosinski, Psychological Science, March 2017

Part of the three-month class involved getting together between sessions in the homes of various group members, talking about how each person had been raised to think about money. They also shared their faith stories and what—if any—impact that had on how they viewed spending and saving. "The people in my group became friends," recalls Brad. "I still get together with some of them even though the class ended years ago. We never would have met if someone hadn't intentionally thrown us together."

Small groups help us figure out who we are in Christ

Small groups are great places to explore faith and sort out what it looks like to follow Jesus. In your small group you can help people share their faith stories, grapple with confusion about the Bible, or make connections between Bible truth and daily life.

Plus, small groups are top-notch places for sharing meals and laughter.

When the church was just firing up, here's how those early Christians lived:

> *They devoted themselves to the apostles' teaching and to fellowship, to the breaking of bread and to prayer. Everyone was filled with awe at the many wonders and signs performed by the apostles. All the believers were together and had everything in common. They sold property and possessions to give to anyone who had need. Every day they continued to meet together in the temple courts. They broke bread in their homes and ate together with glad and sincere hearts, praising God and enjoying the favor of all the people. And the Lord added to their number daily those who were being saved.* (Acts 2:42-47)

They spent time in corporate worship as well as gathering in homes for more intimate fellowship. Large groups and small groups.

God values relationships

God values community—it's part of God's very nature. That God is in himself a community of three persons (Father, Son, and Holy Spirit) may be baffling but somehow it's true—and it's working. God exists in a perfect state of unity, something Jesus urges us to desire while praying in John 17:1

Small groups are a place unity can be tasted, tested, and refined. And that's ultimately the "why" of small groups: loving relationships matter to God and are the currency of his Kingdom.

As you lead your small group you encourage those you lead to enter into community. You're advancing the Kingdom. You're honoring and glorifying God. And together you and your group are preparing for an eternity in heaven, a place defined by relationship with God.

So embrace your role as a small group leader with enthusiasm! Ask God to lead you as you dive into facilitating your group, relying on him every step of the way.

CHAPTER 2

WHAT SORT OF SMALL GROUP
ARE YOU LEADING?

*N*ick was delighted to be asked by his pastor to lead a small group. Years before, in another church, a small group had supported Nick through a painful divorce. "They were my lifeline," remembers Nick. "Looking back, I'd say they saved my life."

Coming out of his divorce Nick realized he had a serious inability to set healthy boundaries. Figuring he wasn't alone in that, Nick quietly let his church friends know he'd be leading a group focused on setting appropriate, godly boundaries.

Nick was right about the need. Eight people wanted in. They agreed to meet on Sunday evenings. Nick ordered copies of a book he'd found helpful, and everything looked rosy, right up until Nick reported back to his pastor—who quickly rained on his parade.

The pastor had envisioned a group that studied the Gospels, the expectation being group members would invite non-believing friends and neighbors to meetings. When the group hit twenty members it would divide and then those two groups would spin off to repeat the process.

The pastor thought small groups should be about evangelism. Nick was all about personal spiritual growth. Nick still launched his small group but not as an "official" ministry of the congregation.

"My group worked through the book, held each other accountable, and made significant progress," recalls Nick. "But when the church listed small group options, we weren't included. I clearly wasn't doing small groups the right way."

15

Neither Nick or his pastor was wrong, they just envisioned two very different types of small group. Nick wanted to lead a group focused on personal growth and care; his pastor doubled down on outreach.

Avoid a similar disconnect by having a frank conversation with your church's small group ministry leadership about what your group is expected to be and accomplish. How's that line up with what you feel called to do? Are your gifts, interests, and schedule a match?

Whether in your church they're called Small Groups, Life Groups, Care Groups, Koinonia Groups, Cell Groups, Growth Groups, Discipleship Groups, or *Those People Who Meet At Karen's House*, you need to answer those questions. Until you do, you may land where Nick landed.

The following is a list of some small group models, though the names sometimes vary. If the approach to groups where you serve is either flexible or undetermined, these categories can serve as a launch pad for a discussion with the small group ministry leadership at your church and be helpful in clarifying your thinking.

• Open Group

This group has no limit on the number of people who can join, and new members are welcome at any time.

Pros: The flexibility of this model makes it easy for new church members and those exploring Christianity to have a small group experience, which may usher them into the faith and/or your church.

Cons: Groups can grow so large the intimacy wanted in a small group disappears. The shifting membership may diminish commitment to the group.

Considerations: You'll have a lot of follow-up to do with individuals who come and go. Study materials that assume frequent attendance aren't suitable.

• Closed Group

This group limits the number of participants, at least for a specific period of time. Once the group is formed, no new members are allowed.

Pros: This format helps trust deepen and members hold one another accountable. This model is often used when the focus is deep discipleship, or confidentiality is valued.

Cons: A closed group can forget about evangelism as others aren't allowed to join. Groups may also become (or be perceived as) cliques.

Considerations: This type of group places a premium on commitment (including yours).

• Bible Study Group

This group uses the Bible and/or study guides to work through a portion (usually an individual book) of the Bible.

Pros: Group members deep dive into scripture and, if using a study guide, can take turns leading the group. Meetings have a predictable structure.

Cons: These groups may start to feel like a class. Members with little Bible knowledge may feel insecure or embarrassed. And study books can get expensive.

Considerations: Picking the right study material is critical. (See Chapter 19 for help.)

• Seeker-Centered Group

This group is designed to help non-believers investigate God and, hopefully, embrace both God and your church.

Pros: Tightly focused on evangelism, group members are united in purpose. Impact is easy to measure and results visible.

Cons: Session content is often limited to addressing common obstacles to faith commitment. Deeper intimacy and accountability may not happen because group participants frequently change.

Considerations: You'll need to graciously accept, without judgement, "non-Christian" behavior and language from faith-explorers. Also, you'll cover introductory lessons only.

• Affiliation Group

This group forms around a hobby or interest. Those in a church who enjoy riding motorcycles, working out, or stargazing form a group to pursue their passion together. A spiritual component is added through a brief devotion or scripture reading.

Pros: Shared interests are a natural springboard for conversation. It's easy for group members to invite non-believers who share the mutual interest.

Cons: Some participants may care more about the activity than any spiritual content. Some activities aren't conducive to conversation (a motorcycle run, for instance) or the activity is seasonal. Commitment to the group is generally low.

Considerations: You've got to be truly passionate about the activity involved. Group membership will likely be transitory, making ongoing discipleship and mentoring challenging.

• Neighborhood Group

This is group membership is based on geography.

Pros: Living in close proximity makes it easier for group members to enjoy spontaneous dinner dates and over-the-fence conversations. Basing group membership on geography alone often creates multi-generational groups.

Cons: Neighborhoods may be populated with people in a similar demographic, making diversity a challenge. Strictly enforcing geography can separate friends and limit options for group members.

Considerations: These groups can be especially effective for evangelism, as meeting invites are to join neighbors rather than strangers.

• Sermon-Review Group

This group reviews the past Sunday's sermon, exploring the same topic or digging deeper into the sermon's scripture text.

Pros: Revisiting sermons reinforces their message. A sermon-review group also encourages Sunday attendance.

Cons: Not all church members attend every week, so some group members won't hear the sermons. Small group material must be created and made available in advance, limiting the pastor's flexibility to change up a sermon topic at the last moment.

Considerations: Some sermons won't feel relevant to all group members. You're limited as to what will be discussed at meetings. And your church has to make sermons available, preferably on a website, for small group members who didn't hear the sermon live.

• Issue-Oriented Group

These groups, which are often closed, deal with issues that likely require confidentiality. Recovery and Parenting Strong-Willed Kids groups are examples of issue-oriented groups.

Pros: Members value the group because it addresses an immediate, felt need. Groups are usually accountability-based and the transparency required often leads to supportive friendships forming.

Cons: It's easy to burn out leading these high-intensity groups, so setting personal boundaries is important. Members dealing with some issues may require support their entire lives, which is likely well be beyond the scope of your small group.

Considerations: Check with your church staff to find out if leading this group makes you a mandatory reporter. You'll have to enforce confidentiality, which can be a challenge. You'll be most effective leading if you have previous experience with the issue at hand and also have a counseling background.

• Service-Focused Group

This group consists of volunteers involved in an area of service within the church (ushering, children's ministry, lay counseling) or preparing for short- or long-term mission trips.

Pros: Shared tasks are opportunities to talk about life as members travel or serve together. The purpose of the group is clear: to accomplish a specific task.

Cons: Some tasks make sharing difficult. If the traffic-control team is in the coffee shop praying together you'll soon have fender-benders out in the parking lot.

Considerations: Leading this group includes providing ongoing task training. There's often little opportunity for Biblical depth. At best, you'll have a team huddle allowing you to pray together and, perhaps, share a brief devotional thought.

Selecting a small group model *before* you launch your group lets you clearly describe what your group will be about and what resources, if any, group members are expected to provide. Making those decisions up front lets you draw to your group people who are hungry for what you have to offer.

CHAPTER 3

ANATOMY OF A HEALTHY GROUP

*S*mall groups are sometimes referred to as "cell groups." It's a fitting name when considering what makes your small group healthy.

A cell is the smallest structural unit of an organism capable of functioning independently (note: this *will* be on the final exam). Cells have lives of their own, contributing to the health—or illness—of the larger organism.

Healthy cells keep host organisms vibrant and robust. But toxic cells (think cancer) can cripple and kill their host. The same can be said of small groups and your church, which means you want lead the healthiest small group possible.

Small group expert Rick Howerton has seen his share of small groups, both the healthy and toxic varieties. He suggests if you want a healthy, fully-functioning group you've got to build in four components.

"In a healthy group you'll see theological, relational, restorational, and missional elements in play," says Howerton. "All four are important."

The theological component is a focus on Bible study and application of biblical truth. Your group needs to have a healthy respect for God's Word and allow the Bible inform who you are.

The relational component refers to how group members relate to one another. "In a healthy group you'll see individual members thinking of and meeting the needs of others before they address their own needs," says Howerton.

Restoration happens when members of your group address brokenness in whatever form it presents itself. You may seek to restore failing marriages, deal with painful pasts, or salvage fractured friendships. "A healthy group seeks restoration through the power of God and community," Howerton says. Healthy small groups can become places of deep, profound healing.

Missional groups evangelize and connect with the community. This outward focus prompts invitations to join the group, and expresses itself through service projects, or finds other ways to share the Gospel.

Emphasizing one component more than the others changes the flavor of a small group. "If a group stresses the theological component, you have a Sunday school class," says Howerton. "If the emphasis is on the relational aspect, you have a friendship-focused small group."

Whatever the mix of the four components, Howerton suggests that together they form the foundation of a healthy small group, which means if your small group is healthy, here are ten things you'll see:

You're meeting frequently

"Each group's personality is determined by the personalities of individuals who come and come consistently," says Howerton. "If groups meet infrequently, that group's personality never forms.

"Group members won't know if it's safe to be vulnerable and, if they're not vulnerable, they can't know or meet each other's needs. Nor will they be encouraging one another to grow spiritually."

To stay healthy, how often should your group meet? In part that depends on how much sharing and accountability you want to see. Generally speaking, the more often you meet, the more intimate the sharing. Support groups typically meet weekly. Bible study groups may meet every other week.

Healthy groups meet as often as necessary to fulfill their purpose.

There's authenticity and transparency

It takes time—often months—before sharing in a group moves past the "I'm fine, how about you?" stage. But when it does, that's when groups become truly valuable.

"I can vividly remember the first time someone in my group paused, took a deep breath, and said, 'Can I be honest? I'm falling apart,'" says Donna. "That's the day my small group started to matter to me."

Even small groups focused primarily on Bible study have a relational component. In any healthy small group there's a growing sense of friendship and honesty.

Members become more loving, as well as more knowledgeable

In a healthy group Bible knowledge is paired with deepening spiritual maturity. Group members apply what they're learning and become more patient and accepting of one another. You'll hear about group members connecting over a cup of coffee outside of your group meetings. You'll find it increasingly difficult to "get down to business" at meetings because group members are authentically happy to see and catch up with one another.

Your group is inclusive

Unless your group is by intent a closed group, one mark of health is having a welcome mat perpetually on the porch for newcomers. In addition to your committed core members, you'll meet new attendees who were invited by your group. And those newcomers will be greeted with both enthusiasm and interest. A healthy group is a growing group—both in terms of faith and friendships.

You serve together

You serve—both within and beyond your group. No matter the different ways groups choose to serve one another and others, serving together will help your group grow closer together.

You're raising up new leaders and spinning off new groups

This sign of health begins with you as the leader. It's up to you to identify and build the skills of group members who can themselves lead a group. And when the time is right—your group has outgrown your living room or you've received a nudge from Jesus—you'll spin off a new group.

Everyone has a role to fill

In a healthy group, members all have opportunities to invest in the group. It may be hosting, teaching, making coffee, helping lead, praying, or keeping track of birthdays. If someone is part of your group for more than six weeks and still isn't sure why she would be missed if she dropped out, take action. Ask her to take a job that's both valuable and in line with her gifts and interests, and then honor her service.

The Bible is open—often

Ask any restaurant worker: There's always a group of retired guys who meet on Friday mornings to drink coffee, debate, and fix what's wrong with the world. They laugh, challenge one another, and wouldn't miss meeting for anything. You won't find a more supportive, engaged small group—but they may not be growing spiritually.

Spiritual growth comes with exploring God's Word and then letting it shape your conversations, commitments, and relationships. Is your group digging into the meat of the Bible, and prayerfully asking God to shape you?

Your group is praying

You're praying for one another and your concerns during group meetings and between meetings. In a healthy group you'll hear members checking back with one another about previously shared concerns. You'll hear heartfelt prayers prompted by deep caring and confidence in God's grace.

You're a bit uncomfortable...in a good way

As group leader, you're aware God wants to use your group to literally change lives. But how? What's God up to? How can you cooperate with God's purposes? If asking those questions doesn't keep you in a state of anticipation as you seek God's guidance, you're not paying attention. A healthy group has a leader eager to be led by God, and ready and willing to go wherever God leads.

The definition of health—for an actual cell or a cell group—is that there's life, sustainability, and well-being. How you lead plays a critical role in whether those three attributes are present in your group.

But this isn't all on you. God is willing and able to give you the wisdom, humility, and motivation to lead, and lead well.

Pause now to ask God to equip you to be the leader he wants you to be.

SECTION 2

THE WHO OF SMALL GROUPS

CHAPTER 4

QUALITIES OF A SMALL GROUP LEADER

*A*t first the Apostle Paul was better known for killing Christ-followers than making them. Stephen's first big sermon ended with him being stoned to death. Moses was so unsure about his leadership ability he told God to forget about that whole "set my people free" assignment.

God used them all anyway. And even if you're questioning whether you're ready to lead a small group, God will use you, too… if you'll let him.

The truth is there's no such thing as a perfect or perfectly-prepared small group leader. There *are* qualities that mark effective leaders, so as you prepare to lead ask God to grow these qualities in you:

Attentive to and reliant on God

You may be coming to small group leadership with an impressive set of skills. And a theology degree. And twenty years of experience. None of that matters if you aren't doing what matters most: asking God what he wants to do in and through your small group and then relying on God to do it as you yield to him.

Underline that last sentence because you can accomplish nothing of importance apart from God's power and leading.

"I'm a planner," says Susan, a women's group leader. "I always had a spreadsheet outlining what to talk about at every meeting throughout the entire quarter. At least, that's how I used to do things."

To be truthful, Susan still operates that way. But she now holds her plans with less of an iron-fisted grip.

"I've learned you've got to be willing to shift gears," she says. "You've got to be open to getting a nudge from the Holy Spirit to hit 'pause' and dig deeper into a topic if it's resonating with your group. Maybe you won't cover all the lesson material, but what you cover will be the exact right material."

Susan suggests you listen for the still, small voice of God as you lead. If you feel led to pause or to head a different direction during your meeting, go with it—even if it means abandoning your carefully prepared lesson.

Humility

Wise leaders recognize they aren't the *only* leader in their groups.

God has gifted each person in your group and, at one time or another, every group member may lead a discussion or influence where your group is headed.

Michael Fleming, who's explored and led small groups for decades, reminds leaders "your goal isn't to direct the group. Your goal is to find out where the Lord wants your group to go, and the Lord might be speaking through someone besides you."

It's easy for designated small group leaders (that's you) to be seen as the smartest, most important person in the room. After all, you're the designated "leader." Meetings don't start until you arrive. You meet with the small group coordinator.

"But in the Kingdom we're brothers and sisters," says Fleming. "We're iron sharpening iron, co-leaders serving one another and helping each another grow."

Fleming suggests the designated leader (you again) help everyone in the group embrace their identity in Christ: They're filled with the Spirit, gifted, and have the responsibility to look for where the Lord might be leading your group. If they hear something, it's essential they speak up.

If that sounds like it might get messy, you're right: it can. But it also helps everyone in your group learn to hear and obey the Lord's voice.

Balanced

As a small group leader you'll forever be balancing people and tasks. Your tasks are important and may include contacting group members, leading meetings, organizing service projects—it can be a long list.

Then there are people, the members of your small group. They'll call at inconvenient times, forget commitments, or fail to follow through. They will interrupt your meetings with distracting comments or a loud yawn. They'll get in the way of you crossing everything off your small group to-do list.

But keep this in mind: *People are eternal, tasks are temporary.* If it comes down to baking brownies for the meeting or helping people cope with life, people always win.

Shepherd-Hearted

All those qualities the Bible says should be found in church leaders (1 Timothy 3:1-7; Titus 1:5-9) also apply to you. Why? Because you serve as a shepherd, keeping an eye on the spiritual health of your group's members.

Don't panic. Other than Jesus, there's no perfect shepherd. Every small group leader lets the ball drop sometimes, no small group leader is without sin or sports a halo. The issue isn't your perfection, but God's faithfulness—and your willingness to care for your group members.

Pray for each person in your group and let them know you're praying. When someone mentions a specific need or concern circle back a week later and ask what happened. Connect with people over coffee, outside the group, to find out more about their lives.

Shepherds get to know their individual sheep—go thou and do likewise.

Prepared

Effective small group leaders don't "wing it."

They show up to meetings with an agenda and stick to it unless there's a need to adjust. They highlight their leaders' guide so they aren't glued to the book as they lead. They have the room set up and ready before the first group member shows up.

In short: they *prepare*. They're ready to lead—physically, emotionally, and spiritually. All of this is easier if you use a checklist (see Chapter 24) until getting ready for a meeting is second nature. And then keep using the checklist—it guarantees consistent excellence.

Accepting

Your group becomes a safe place for transparency when judgment is kept to a minimum. Yes, you should challenge wrong actions and attitudes, but speak that truth in love. It's one thing to say, "You're wrong and need to change," and another to say "I'm wondering what you think a faithful next step would be." That first response elicits defensiveness; the second invites a conversation leading to confession and grace.

Remember: you can accept someone without endorsing their behavior or opinions. So create space for growth by not being overly quick to condemn or correct. Instead, respectfully encourage a group member to consider what the Bible or the rest of your group has to say.

As a leader, take Galatians 6:1-3 to heart:

Brothers and sisters, if someone is caught in a sin, you who live by the Spirit should restore that person gently. But watch yourselves, or you also may be tempted. Carry each other's burdens, and in this way you will fulfill the law of Christ. If anyone thinks they are something when they are not, they deceive themselves.

Committed

Group leaders are all in. You show up regularly, even if attendance is sparse. You pray for group members even if they're not praying for you.

When leading is your sweet spot, your role as small group leader energizes. You embrace it as a calling and consider it a privilege. You ask God to give you a heart for your group and let the love shine through your enthusiasm and consistent involvement. And you honestly answer this question: Is there any sin in your life interfering with your leadership role? If so, with the help of God and a trusted friend or two, confess and deal with it.

A Learner

Effective small group leadership involves a number of skills, each of which can deepen with additional training.

Set goals to grow in your ability to listen, in your understanding of scripture, and in facilitating. If your church has a counseling ministry ask for training in how to better listen. No resource in your home church? See what other congregations or community groups (crisis centers often offer listening courses) might sharpen your skills.

Choose to keep learning. Choose to hone your skills.

A Coach

Look for group members to mentor in leadership. Ask them to prayerfully consider if they might be called to be leaders and, if so, give them the self-assessment at the end of Chapter Then, if they're open to leading, give them responsibilities within the group and provide feedback about how they're doing.

When the time is right, help them get their own group up and running.

Encouraging and Empowering

Small group leaders watch for what God is doing in group members and celebrate it. They affirm the growth they see and choose to trust more growth is coming.

As a leader you value "we" more than "me." You don't insist on running the show yourself, instead letting group members also shape the group. Recognizing God is at work in all of you, you grant each group member the appropriate respect.

Expectant

Call it "divine anticipation." You look to God, expecting he'll bless your leadership and your group. You pray with expectation God will answer. You view the future not as a spooky territory out on the horizon but as a place in which God will do remarkable things.

When you're expecting God to show up, it's astounding how often he does just that—in your life and the lives of your group members.

Unafraid

Unafraid looks like this: You're willing to linger over tough questions. To share your own story if it's helpful to others, including the parts that still sting. To ask God to help you grow as a disciple and a leader.

You lean into spiritual growth and invite others to journey with you.

Passionate about unity

Some churches fear that small groups will go "rogue," teaching half-truths or becoming places unhappy church members gather to complain and criticize.

At times that fear has proven to be justified—but not in your group. As an effective leader you'll be diligent to align your group with the goals and mission of your larger church body. You'll provide a spot that members who are dissatisfied with church leadership can voice their concerns—to a point.

That point is when gossip or accusations begin creeping in. That's when you'll take the conversation off-line, between you and the disgruntled group member. You'll coach a biblical resolution to conflict within the Body of Christ (see Matthew 18:15-18) and facilitate the process if necessary.

As leaders let's protect unity—and guard grace. by regularly seeking the Lord in prayer and intentionally fostering these qualities. By God's grace you'll grow in your capacity as a servant leader.

CHAPTER 5

HOW TO TELL IF YOU'RE LEADING WELL

*I*n taking on a job, be it in the business world or as a small group ministry volunteer, it's helpful to know what's required or expected as a way of being able to assess if you're doing a good job.

One tool that can be helpful is a job description. Another is a self-assessment. If your church already has and provides a small group leader job description, great! If not, the following is a general document that can be used as a starting point and be customized.

You can walk through the following as needed with the person in charge of your church's small group ministry. Ask questions. Get clarity so from the outset you know what's expected of you. Know who you'll report to and when and who to call if something happens you're not sure how to handle.

Small Group Leader Job Description:

Lead and facilitate a group in such a way it promotes healthy relationships, deepens faith in God, and equips and empowers group members for ministry.

Responsible to:

Director of Small Group Ministries

Prerequisites:

1. Must be an active member of First Church

2. Attend small group leadership orientation and subsequent team meetings

3. Affirm First Church's Statement of Beliefs

4. Demonstrate a desire to use spiritual gifts in a small group leadership setting

5. Share and support the vision of First Church to disciple others

6. Have an ability to communicate clearly and well

7. Be teachable

Length of Commitment:
One year, renewable at 11 months

Responsibilities:
1. In conjunction with the Director of Small Group Ministries, craft a vision statement for the group, defining the mission and style of the small group.

2. Select and mentor a Small Group Assistant, the goal being to prepare the assistant to lead another small group.

3. In conjunction with the Assistant, advertise the group and invite potential participants.

4. Convene the group at least twice per month.

5. Prepare meeting agendas including sharing, prayer, Bible content, and application.

6. Organize at least two small group service projects per year.

7. Pray for each group member daily

8. Embrace responsibility for nurturing relationships within the group.

9. Foster a sense of outreach that results in group members extending invitations to adults outside the church to join the group.

10. Meet monthly with the Director of Small Group Ministries (by phone or in person)

11. Notify pastoral staff of crises that arise in the lives of group members that would benefit from a pastoral response.

No, that's not an exact fit for your leadership role, but it covers the basics. A leader with this job description knows what preparation is required, how long the commitment lasts, and what needs to happen. Tasks are clearly spelled out. But those are just the tasks.

Part of leading well involves your group's feelings about how you do those tasks. Are you pleasant? Engaged and engaging? Do they sense you care? Those intangibles are real and can be measured—just not by you.

A suggestion: Occasionally have the Director of Small Group Ministries contact a few group members and, with a promise of confidentiality, ask these three questions:

- What does (your name here) do well as a leader in your small group?
- What could (your name here) do better?
- If you could change one thing about your group, what would it be?

When the person who does these interviews sums up the answers for you, you're getting an unfiltered look at how you're perceived—and what changes you might want to make. Receive this feedback humbly and prayerfully act on it. Also remember to ask God how you're doing. How well you perform your small group leader role is ultimately far less important than how well you step out of the way to let God do what God does. You can stumble your way through a lesson and God can still use the passage you present to transform a life.

This isn't all about you. It's about God.

"I find it comforting that God spoke through Balaam's donkey (Numbers 22:21-39), " says our friend, Nick. (Numbers 22:21-39) "I figure that even on my worst day, when I show up late to group, left my notes at the office, and I'm half-asleep, God can still use me. I just have to be willing." Amen.

Finally, when you ask a group member to fill a role, provide a job description. You probably don't need to get into the details of execution, but be sure there's a clear understanding of expectations. To save you time, sample job descriptions for common small group roles are in Chapter 25 to use and adapt.

The following actions and attitudes self-assessment is another tool that can help you identify particular areas of strength, as well as practices to improve on as a small group leader.

The problem is we often don't perceive ourselves accurately. So talk through your answers with someone you trust and who knows you well. Does that person agree or disagree with your ratings? Why?

Your conversation will affirm where you're doing well and where there's room to grow.

Self-Assessment

Circle the number that best represents your response to the statement. Don't overthink your response—your initial response is often the most accurate.

Use this ranking system:

Strongly agree

Agree

Neutral

Disagree

Strongly disagree

1. I pray for myself regularly. (1...2...3...4...5)
2. I pray for others regularly. (1...2...3...4...5)
3. I believe God wants me to serve as a small group leader. (1...2...3...4...5)
4. There is a pattern of ongoing sin in one or more areas of my life. (1...2...3...4...5)
5. I'm known as a caring person, quick to serve others. (1...2...3...4...5)
6. I regularly read the Bible for my own spiritual formation. (1...2...3...4...5)
7. If my church leaders knew the real me, they'd still ask me to lead a group. (1...2...3...4...5)
8. I can coach others to learn what I know. (1...2...3...4...5)
9. I listen well. (1...2...3...4...5)
10. I believe God can speak to me through other people. (1...2...3...4...5)
11. I'm tolerant of others' thoughts and opinions. (1...2...3...4...5)
12. I'm reliable and follow through on commitments. (1...2...3...4...5)
13. I've learned to hear God's voice. (1...2...3...4...5)
14. I can gently confront others when there's truth they need to hear. (1...2...3...4...5)
15. My personal beliefs align with my church's statement of faith. (1...2...3...4...5)
16. I'm known to prepare well for meetings and presentations. (1...2...3...4...5)
17. I'm growing spiritually and can point to evidence of that growth. (1...2...3...4...5)
18. I frequently encourage others. (1...2...3...4...5)

19. I have bandwidth in my life to be a small group leader.
    (1...2...3...4...5)
20. I'm confident God wants me to lead a group.
    (1...2...3...4...5)

CHAPTER 6

RECRUITING OTHERS TO JOIN YOUR GROUP

*Y*our first task as a small group leader is to find people to join your group. But in a world where people seem reluctant to commit to much, how do you do that?

It's helpful if your church actively promotes small groups, speaking about their value from the pulpit, organizing sign-up Sundays, and filling the church website with photos of small groups having fun and changing lives.

But what if that doesn't do the trick? How can you own the task of building your group yourself? Besides, you're not just after people. You're after the *right* people, people drawn to your group's vision and purpose. How do you find and recruit *them*?

Start by answering a few questions:

Who do I want to reach?

This is where your covenant is helpful. If you've described your group's vision and purpose, it will suggest who's likely to have their needs met in your group. For instance, if you're recruiting for a women's group, don't promote it in the Grandpas For God Karate Group.

What's in it for small group members?

Carter Moss has been filling living rooms with people for 25 years, and has this suggestion for putting people in those empty chairs.

"Make your small group valuable because valuable is what people make time for," says Moss. "Find out what people are craving. If it's relational connection, design your group so there's plenty of time to hang out and be real. Other people may want to do a deep dive into scripture and learn new things. If that's the case, deliver that."

You can't be all things to all people, so prayerfully land on a vision and stick with it, even if it's one no other group has tried. Moss is part of a group run by a guy who dubbed the group, "What Would Jesus Barbeque?"

"The leader is really good at tying food into a Bible story," says Moss. "We met last night to make wood fired pizzas so we talked about Shadrach, Meshach, and Abednego in the fiery furnace. I invited a couple friends and they'd already heard about the group and couldn't wait to give it a try."

How will you promote your small group?

Consider promoting your group in any of the following ways. In fact, consider promoting your group through *all* of them:

• **Tell people at church about the group.** Briefly share the vision and ask if the person standing in front of you knows anyone who might want to get involved.

• **Deputize group members to find new members.** Unless your group is closed, make it a group project to grow and, eventually, multiply. Since people tend to hang out with people like themselves, if Nancy enjoys the group she'll likely have friends who will, too. Nothing beats a personal invitation.

• **Encourage church staff to be part of a small group.** Not only are staff great people to recruit for your group, but they'll have stories to share about small groups from the stage, in social media, and elsewhere. Those stories all enhance the perception that groups like yours are valuable.

- **Ask for two minutes in the pulpit.** Talk about your group or small groups in general. Include an invitation to participate.
- **Insert a general invitation into the church bulletin or website.** Consider setting up an information table by the church door, too. Or send out some emails to the church list once you've got permission to do so.
- **Reach out to non-Christian friends and neighbors.** (Assuming non-believers are welcome to your group, of course.)
- **Capitalize on timing.** "People seem more open to starting things in January and September," says Moss. "Even when they don't have kids, people tend to fall into the school calendar." Moss's advice: plan promotions during these times.

Decide: What's the next step?

When someone is interested, what do you want that person to do? Sign a form? Have lunch with you? Attend a meeting to check out the group?

If attending is what you're after, offer this assurance: Coming once doesn't mean someone is committed forever. There's no pressure to join, just an invitation. You won't be offended if someone tries your group and decides it's not for them.

Once a visitor has checked out your group and it's time to transition that person from "guest" to "member," here are three ways to bring that visitor in for a landing:

- **Coffee and conversation.** After people attend twice, ask them to meet you at a local coffee shop. Share your story, hear theirs, and answer any questions they have.
- **Adopt a guest.** Ask an established group member to "adopt" a new attendee, sitting with the person and connecting the newbie to other group members. This goes a long way toward easing someone into an existing group.

• **Pray.** God knows if a visitor would be blessed by being in your group. Invite God to speak to visitors about whether they're a fit—in your group or another one.

Now Get Busy

If you start you group with just a few people, that's fine. Keep talking, keep inviting, and keep praying and you'll soon find yourself needing to borrow extra chairs to seat everyone.

And you'll need more cookies, too!

SECTION 3

THE HOW OF LEADING
A THRIVING SMALL GROUP

CHAPTER 7

SMALL GROUP GROUND RULES AND SAMPLE COVENANT

*J*enny enjoyed visiting her friend's small group Bible study.

"Everyone was so nice," she remembers. "People introduced themselves, they paid attention when I spoke, they even laughed at my lame jokes."

So of course Jenny returned the following week, and the week after that. But then her shift changed at the restaurant where she waited tables and she didn't show up at the next meeting.

That's when the calls started.

"First I heard from my friend who wondered why I'd missed," says Jenny. "I apologized for not letting her know and figured that would be the end of it. It wasn't."

Jenny got a call from the small group leader expressing disappointment she'd quit the group. Jenny hadn't realized she'd actually joined it; she thought the study was a come-when-you-can arrangement.

"I heard from the guy three more times, and each time he piled on more guilt," says Jenny. "They were concerned. They were praying for me. A couple of the women in the group wanted to come talk about my spiritual condition."

When Jenny's schedule changed again and she could have returned, she didn't. "No way was I going back," Jenny says.

No, the group wasn't a cult. Jenny says they were just big on accountability but nobody had explained that to her. Had she known, she'd have been clear from the start she couldn't make a commitment because her work shifts changed often.

A covenant—a document spelling out what was expected of people who attended that group—could have saved everyone time and aggravation.

Avoid encountering your own Jenny moment by creating a covenant for your group, preferably before you start looking for small group participants. If you're leading an existing group, realize that whatever is currently happening in the group is probably what you'll have to live with. At best you can bring a covenant to your group and talk about whether the group is willing to embrace its expectations and standards.

A covenant does several things well: It clarifies expectations and ground rules, stating them in clear, concise language. It becomes a document you can point to if someone in your group fails to adhere to those ground rules.

Your covenant shouldn't look and feel like a legally-binding contract. Just write out what's important, keeping it simple. A sample is at the end of this chapter for your reference. It won't fit your situation exactly but will save you time as you revise it.

What you include in your covenant is up to you (and/or your small group director) but the following are points that are often addressed:

A Description of Your Group's Purpose

Are you a Bible study or a rock-climbing affiliation group? Is your group open or closed? Describing your small group and stating its purpose will help draw the appropriate people to your group and keep your group on track.

Commitment

If engaging as fully as possible in group discussions and activities is important, say so. No, it won't always be possible for each person to attend every meeting. Nor will everyone always have something to say at a meeting. But set the expectation that everyone has freedom to speak, and is encouraged to do so. If you'll occasionally serve together, mention that.

Also spell out who to call prior to a meeting if attendance isn't possible.

A Culture of Respect

Declare your group a place where there's shared respect, and indicate that respect looks like this: clear, kind, communication. Everyone's thoughts and doubts are welcome, their stories embraced. Group members show up on time prepared and ready to listen to one another and God. There's a sincere effort to participate fully, serving and blessing other group members.

Discussion Ground Rules

We live in a contentious world. Keep that from infecting your group by agreeing up front to not avoid polarizing topics but to address them in a healthy way. Set the bar for conversation so group members listen well, assume best intentions, and speak their truths directly, gently, and in love.

Confidentiality

Be clear that what's shared at group needs to stay at group. Be explicit about this ground rule: trust and transparency won't grow if people fear being quoted outside the group. Unless a group member gives explicit permission for his or her story or situation to be shared outside your group, assume it's confidential. Exceptions should be if someone threatens harm to themselves or others, or if an intent to commit a crime is shared. Should that occur, as leader it's your responsibility to immediately inform others.

Accountability

If your group will encourage discipleship, let group members know they have permission to speak into one another's lives as they believe the Lord leads. Mutual accountability is a skill many small group members lack, so expect to do some coaching along the way.

Preparation

If you'll use materials requiring outside reading, make note of it. Otherwise, participants may show up not having done their "homework" and discussions will be difficult.

Proactive Communication

When a snowstorm blows through and might bump your meeting off the calendar on short notice, how will people know? Include a process or person by which that information is available.

Group Duration

When signing on to be in a small group it's reassuring to know there's an exit ramp. State a date when group members can be blessed as they leave, or re-up to stay in the group. Use that time to honestly evaluate the direction of the group; is it time to make an adjustment? To shift the official leadership?

Sample Covenant (Revise as you wish):

Purpose:

I recognize our small group is outward focused—open to new members as the Lord adds them. And I acknowledge our intent is to become more mature followers of Jesus.

To that end I'll explore the Bible, applying its truth to my life. I'll also seek to maintain healthy, encouraging relationships with group members, seeking to serve and build them up.

Commitment

Because God works through all group members, I promise to do my best to be present for group meetings and events. I'll participate as fully as possible in discussions and group decisions.

If I can't attend a scheduled meeting or event I'll call the designated person to let the group know I won't be there.

A Culture of Respect

I'll treat other group members with respect. That includes how I communicate, how I participate, and how I speak of the group. I'll show up on time and seek to support and encourage the group.

Discussion Ground Rules

I agree to listen well, offering advice sparingly and only when requested. I'll encourage others, support others, and speak the truth in love. I'll address conflicts quickly and with the goal of reconciliation.

Confidentiality

I understand what's shared at group stays at group. This includes anything shared in person, electronically, by phone, or in any other way. The exception: If I'm married I can share with my spouse unless the group member sharing indicates otherwise.

I will help our group be a safe place, one where trust grows.

Accountability

I give other group members permission to speak into my life, and to call on me when I'm needed. I'll also risk sharing with others in the group what I feel the Lord has for me to say.

Preparation

I'll prepare any necessary materials or complete any necessary reading before group meetings so I can better participate in discussions.

Proactive Communication

If I have any question about whether scheduled meetings or events might be cancelled because of weather or other reasons, I'll call the designated contact person to check.

Group Duration

I understand on or about [DATE] the group will celebrate what God's done in our group and at that time I'm invited to renew my commitment to the group for another year. I can also leave with the group's blessing. At that celebration meeting I'll help explore how we might better achieve our purpose, or what new purpose the Lord might have for us.

CHAPTER 8

YOUR FIRST MEETING

*I*t's here: your first meeting!

To make sure it's a first meeting that encourages people to return for a second one, here are three big picture issues to consider, plus a list of specific items to address.

First, the big picture items:

Check the space

The meeting space can make or break your small group before it starts. That's what Pat Sikora discovered when she launched a mom's Bible study at her church.

"We met in a large fellowship hall and I wanted to be sure there was room for everyone," says Sikora, who set the room up with rows of chairs.

At the first meeting Sikora enthusiastically greeted the crowd sitting in tidy rows facing her. "I said, 'Isn't this wonderful? Isn't this great?' And all I got was blank stares. It felt like we slogged through the whole meeting."

The same thing happened at the second meeting. And the third.

"Finally I said, 'This isn't my Bible study—it's yours. You have to own it. If you don't, it won't work. I need you to be engaged.' But yet again: blank stares."

The next week, while ministry leaders were in the back room praying, participants got engaged. *Really* engaged.

"I came out and they'd rearranged the room," says Sikora "Chairs were in circles around tables so the room was more conversational. There was no more looking at the back of someone's head." For Sikora, it was lesson learned as she moved forward as a small group leader. Two lessons learned, actually.

"The first lesson was to give people ownership. To make sure people knew they can change things, or at least suggest changes. In that mom's group nobody thought they had the authority to re-do the seating until I gave them permission. You have to let people have a voice."

"And, second, you *must* pay attention to your physical space. The room arrangement was squelching conversation. Once the gals got it the way they wanted it, we were off and running."

Have and use an agenda

Especially in a new group, an agenda keeps you on track. Announcing your agenda helps people relax, too, because they know what's coming. Some group leaders use the following as a simple one-hour agenda:

• **Gathering**: This is when group members arrive, find seats, and connect in casual conversation. It's also when you serve refreshments so if a group member is late all that person misses is the Doritos. Allow 10 to 15 minutes.

• **Meeting Content**: If your group is primarily a Bible study, this is the lesson and application time. Allow 30 minutes.

• **Sharing Life**: Here's where the group checks in regarding previous prayer requests, shares challenges, and provides support and encouragement. It's also when you pray for one another. Allow about 15 minutes.

Once you have a steady rhythm in place, you'll be able to easily adjust the amount of time you spend in each part of your agenda.

But don't carve your agenda in stone, because you never know what will happen during any given meeting. Nick remembers a meeting where the group began to weep softly.

"During the lesson a woman started crying. I signaled the leader to pause, but he kept on going. I finally interrupted, asking the woman if she wanted to share what was happening either with the whole group or with just one other person in another room.

"She shook her head as she reached for another tissue so the leader plowed ahead.

"To this day I'm ashamed I didn't persist, gently asking again if she wanted to share. She later told me she'd just discovered her husband was having an affair and desperately wanted the group to hug her and pray for her. But when she saw the leader hurrying through the lesson she didn't want to get in the way."

Have an agenda, but hold it in an open palm.

God might have a different agenda in mind.

Pray: a lot

Pray for people you expect to show up for your meeting. Ask God to orchestrate conversations and that everyone in the group will grow.

Pray for your leadership, asking God to help you lead from a place of dependence on him. Pray for wisdom and discernment.

Pray for your own spiritual condition. It's easier for God to use you if the two of you are attuned, so confess sin in your life and seek forgiveness. Commit your skills and gifts to God, asking him to use you to be a blessing to others.

You can't pray too much or too often as you prepare for your first meeting.

And every meeting after that.

When it comes to items that will help your first meeting come off without a hitch, consider these:

Make your first meeting relational

Even if people already know one another, they don't know one another in this new context. Rather than dive into a study, take the time for people to introduce themselves. Who are they, what do they enjoy, what are they hoping to get from the group?

Give everyone in the circle two minutes to provide basic information.

Be prepared—and show it

Your first meeting sets the tone for everything that follows. "It's where you communicate that the people who've come are important and you've planned and prepared for them," says Sikora.

Your preparation shines through how you prepare the meeting area, whether you start on time, and what you have to say as the meeting launches.

Share your vision and the group covenant

Set the basic ground rules for your group. Let everyone know expectations about involvement and confidentiality, whether it's a closed or open group, how decisions will be made.

Turn on every light in the place

This is what real estate agents do to brighten a room and make it more inviting. Do the same—it makes your house warm and cozy.

Set the temperature

Err on the cool side. Once a dozen people are in the room the temperature will rise. Do a quick "is everyone comfortable?" check about half way through your meeting and adjust as needed.

Think through transportation

Is there adequate parking if an extra dozen cars land on your street? Is there convenient public transportation if you're in an urban area?

Select and play background music

No, not your vintage Mega Metal Death Squad CD. Rather, play something light and instrumental in the background as people arrive. Remember to turn off the music when the meeting is about to begin. Do this consistently over several meetings and fading music will become a soft signal it's time to start.

Catch people at the door

Greet them with a smile and handshake. Let them know that at future meetings they can just let themselves in.

Alternately, leave the door open so it's easy to see others gathered inside.

A caveat: Be sure they know when the meeting is supposed to begin.

"We had a 'just walk on in' policy and one couple got the time wrong and showed up as our family was eating dinner," remembers Nick. "They felt awful but we just pulled up two more chairs to the table and had them join us for desert. It worked out fine."

Circle up

Take heed of what Pat Sikora discovered: seating arranged in circles facilitates conversations and increases intimacy. It also keeps people more engaged because there's no "back of the room."

Name tags. (Really, trust us.)

Even if people see each other often at church, that doesn't mean everyone knows everyone's names. Erase any opportunity for embarrassment by having people fill out name tags.

"If you get pushback, tell that guy who says he knows everyone's name that this isn't for him; it's for those who may not know all the names," says Nick. "It's a service to others."

Set out snacks and beverages

Keep food simple and preferably healthy and have a couple options for beverages. One of those options should always be water, by the way.

Stash the pets

They may be well behaved, but they're still a distraction. And you'd be wise to check if anyone has allergies to pets before you choose to host your meeting in a house with eleven cats in residence.

Have a clock visible

During the meeting don't check your watch or phone. Do what counselors do in their offices: place a clock so you can discretely check the time.

Handle corporate prayer carefully

At your first meeting you don't yet know who's comfortable praying aloud so don't put anyone on the spot. Ask for prayer concerns and then lead a prayer yourself, or ask a volunteer to do so. If you do want everyone to pray, form pairs so it can be just two people praying aloud together.

Start and end on time

"If you begin late you'll train people to be late," says Sikora. "And I wrap up meetings within five minutes of the time I said we'd end. People can hang out if they want, but it's okay to leave, too."

You'll find checklists you can use for your meeting in chapter 2It covers all the basics except for one:

Love the people who come

When people enter a space that's been covered in prayer and they're greeted by a leader who loves them, who cares if the snacks are stale or the chairs wobbly? Your meeting will go fine because you've provided what matters most: love.

CHAPTER 9

WAYS TO OPEN YOUR MEETING

The first five minutes of your meeting transition group members from whatever they've been doing all day to where they are now: gathered together, present for one another, and listening to God.

The last few moments of your meeting are what's top of mind as people walk out the door and back into their daily routine.

Let's pause to consider how you can make the most of opening and closing your meetings.

Opening Your Meeting

The first few minutes of your meeting are the perfect time for group members to get better acquainted and for you to encourage group bonding.

If you've endured one too many cheesy icebreakers in the past, you might be tempted to discount opening activities. But trust us: for at least your first few meetings they're valuable. They'll ease everyone into the meeting, deepen friendships, and form community.

And believe us when we say the following activities work. They're tried, true, and—if properly presented—dairy-free. Not a speck of cheese on them.

Just keep the following in mind...

• **Scale openers so everyone participates.** For instance, if the opener involves sharing stories and your small group has fifteen members, form subgroups of two or three and share stories there.

• **Don't let openers overwhelm your meeting.** Keep them to about five minutes if possible, longer if you see people connecting in powerful ways.

• **Never force participation.** If someone opts out, let it be. That person has a reason.

• **If at all possible, make a connection** between the opener and lesson content. It's okay if openers are just for fun, but they're stronger if they're fun *and* related to what's coming later in the meeting.

• **And enter into these activities believing they'll work.** If you're enthused about an opener, your group will be, too.

That said, here are some winning openers:

Thumbs Up, Thumbs Down

Ask group members to briefly share the best and most challenging events that have happened since you last met. This is typically a longer opener, but it provides insight into the lives of group members. It's can also surface prayer concerns so be on the look-out for them.

For this opener, you go first. Be brief but transparent; you're modeling the sort of response you're looking for from group members.

Discussion Questions

Ask group members a question—preferably a playful one—and see what they say. If you can connect the question to lesson content without too big a stretch, do so.

Ten sample questions to get you started:

- Would you rather be incredibly lucky or very skilled? Why?

- Your happy place: Where is it? What makes it happy?
- If you couldn't live in this country where would you like to live? Why?
- Who's someone you wish you could follow around for a day?
- If you won $40, what would you do with the money? What if it was 40 million?
- You get to declare one new law today. What is it?
- When Hollywood makes a film about your life, who should play you?
- If you could instantly speak any new language, what would it be?
- What memories are evoked by your favorite sentimental piece of clothing?
- What's a game you loved playing as a child? How well would you play it now?

Would You Rather? Questions

Ask your group a "would you rather" question and let people take turns answering and explaining their answers. You'll learn a lot!

Ten sample questions:

- Would you rather experience only summer or winter for the next ten years?
- Would you rather lose your ability to speak or to hear?
- Would you rather have 20 percent more money or 20 percent more free time?
- Would you rather know or not know the date you'll die?
- Would you rather have the ability to fly or to read minds?

- Would you rather be rich doing a job you dislike or poor doing a job you love?
- Would you rather work for yourself or someone else?
- Would you rather live in a world with no coffee or no snack foods?
- Would you rather have a pet rhino or a pet giraffe?
- Would you rather have a "pause" button on your life or a "rewind" button?

If Questions

Same idea as *Would You Rather?* Questions, with a slight variation.

- If you could sit next to Jesus on a plane, what would you talk about?
- If you could be someone else for a week, who would you be?
- If you could ask God any question and get an answer, what would you ask?
- If you could reach anyone in the world on the phone, who would you call?
- If you could get your dream job, what would it be?
- If you could fix one thing in this world, what would it be?
- If you could live over one day in your life, what day would you pick?
- If you could live anywhere but where you live, where would that be?
- If you could see just one color the rest of your life, what's the color?

- If you had to sing a song in public, what song would you pick?

Umbrella Stand

In old black-and-white British movies there was always an umbrella stand by the front door. The butler placed visitors' umbrellas in it when they arrived and gave the umbrellas back when they left.

After your group gathers, ask what things people are dealing with that distract keep them from being fully present during your meeting. Ask people to mentally leave those pressures and issues at the door; they can pick them back up when they leave.

For the duration of the meeting, ask your group to let God soothe their aching hearts and minds.

The following openers can probably be used just once, but they're effective:

Run For It

Tell group members they have just 60 seconds to grab what's most important to save from their homes because a lava flow is coming. People and pets are already in the car; what else would they take—and why?

Be aware some group members may have actually experienced an evacuation because of fire, flooding, or other natural disaster. If that's the case, allow time to hear their stories.

Uncommon Commonalities

This opener is more fun if your group has been together awhile because group members will have to dig deep for responses.

Form trios (separating spouses and besties) and have trios find a minimum of five things they have in common that aren't immediately obvious. Have they all forgotten to renew their driver's licenses? Graduated with honors? Given a gallon of blood? The more unusual the commonality, the bigger the bragging rights.

One and Only

Go around the room asking each person to share something that makes them unique in the room. For instance, they might have met a specific celebrity. Or once sunk a half-court shot while playing basketball. Whatever it is, the rest of the group will report if they've done it, too. And group members will learn about each another.

Flags

Hand out pencils and paper, then ask group members to each draw a flag that symbolizes themselves. They can include any symbols or words they want. Allow two minutes for drawing and then ask group members to take turns showing their flags. Encourage questions.

Faces

On one side of a cheap, uncoated paper plate have group members each draw a mask that captures how they think people see them. Then, on the other side of the plate, draw a face that represents how they see themselves.

Ask group members to take turns displaying both sides of their plates.

Don't do this opener until your group has established trust.

Pennies

Pass around a bowl of coins so every person can take one—without examining the coin closely. Then ask group members to share what was happening in their lives during the year the coin was minted.

Variations: What do you remember caring about during that year? How would you describe your relationship with God during that year? Who was important in your life that year?

Hint: Be sure you include only coins that were minted during the lifespan of participants. If someone picks a coin that predates him or her ask that person to select another coin.

CHAPTER 10

WAYS TO CLOSE YOUR MEETING

Closing your meeting

A good closing activity gives permission to leave but also gives permission to hang out for fellowship. No matter what closer you use (possibilities follow), add an explicit invitation to stick around awhile.

Close With Prayer

It's the default setting for small groups and for good reason: it's a natural transition. You've been focused on one another, now you focus on God, and then—out the door.

But prayer is too important to simply be a signal you're wrapping things up.

If you choose to pray as a closer, try some of the innovative approaches you'll find in Chapter 1They'll keep your group prayer time fresh and memorable.

Elevator Pitch

If your small group focuses on Bible study, ask volunteers to take 20 seconds to sum up the main point of the meeting's study. Ask several people to give it a try and compare responses. Did you all agree?

So What?

Ask your group to respond to this question: what, if anything, did you hear or do at this meeting that will matter in a week? A year? Twenty years?

Now you know what people really heard.

Action Step

If one of your group's goals is discipleship, wrap up your meeting by asking people to turn to partners and describe what they'll do in response to what you talked about together. Ask partners to follow up with one another at your next meeting.

Toddler Time

Again, for Bible study oriented groups, this challenge: sum up what you discovered about the Bible, about God, or about yourself during the meeting in such a way that a 4-year old would understand.

Share a Benediction

Using scripture to bless your group is one way to refocus on God as you end your meeting. Ask group members to cup their hands, bow their heads, or hold hands as the benediction is spoken.

Some suggested benedictions follow:

The Lord bless you and keep you; the Lord make his face shine on you and be gracious to you; the Lord turn his face toward you and give you peace. (Numbers 6:24-26)

May the God who gives endurance and encouragement give you the same attitude of mind toward each other that Christ Jesus had, so that with one mind and one voice you may glorify the God and Father of our Lord Jesus Christ. (Romans 15:5-6)

Now to him who is able to do immeasurably more than all we ask or imagine, according to his power that is at work within us, to him be glory in the church and in Christ Jesus throughout all generations, for ever and ever! Amen. (Ephesians 3:20-21)

May God himself, the God of peace, sanctify you through and through. May your whole spirit, soul and body be kept blameless at the coming of our Lord Jesus Christ. (1 Thessalonians 5:23)

Now may the God of peace, who through the blood of the eternal covenant brought back from the dead our Lord Jesus, that great Shepherd of the sheep, equip you with everything good for doing his will, and may he work in us what is pleasing to him, through Jesus Christ, to whom be glory for ever and ever. Amen. (Hebrews 13:20-21)

Empty Chair

Place an empty chair in the center of your group and ask group members to speak aloud the name of someone, a believer or not-yet-believer, they're asking God to draw to your group to fill that chair.

Then ask God to give your group opportunities to invite those people to your next meeting.

One Word

Ask for volunteers to sum up what they discovered in one word.

Variations: Share a word describing what you'll do as a result of having been at the meeting or how you feel about God right now.

Affirmation Circle

Ask participants to share something they appreciated about someone in the group, citing something that happened during the meeting. It may have been something said, something done, a dazzling smile, or a from-the-heart story that was shared.

A caveat: no one can be affirmed twice until everyone has been affirmed at least once.

And What To Do When Your Group is *Really* Ending

It will happen someday, so be ready.

People move. Schedules shift. Interest wanes. Eventually, your small group will pack it up and ride off into the sunset. The time will come to close it down.

Here's how to handle that event.

• Make sure it's time

Be sure you're reading the situation correctly. Do the members of your group agree that the group has run its course? It's not an admission of failure if you disband—it may be time to do so because God is calling people into other ministries.

If it is time, consider reading together the Bible's description of the disciples watching Jesus ascend to heaven, knowing he's told them to spread out and share the Gospel. Their tightly-knit group was essentially ended. Ask your group: how do they think the disciples felt? What happened as a result of their group splitting apart? How did the disciples remain connected—and how might your group still be connected?

If some of your group's members want to continue meeting together encourage them to form their own group—just without you.

• Look ahead

Pulling the plug on your group isn't something to do on short notice. Give it a month or two so you can discuss all the good things that have come in and through your group. Share memories. Laugh together.

And throw a party. A pull-out-the-stops shindig of gratitude and praise for God's love that you've been privileged to share.

• **Bless each departure**

Pray as a group and then, as group members leave, pray with them individually. Bless them. Thank them. Encourage them. And continue praying for them the next day, week, and month.

CHAPTER 11

THE ART OF FACILITATING A MEETING—
IN PERSON AND OTHERWISE

*Y*ou were asked to lead a small group. The word "Leader" is right there at the top of your job description. You're holding a book for Small Group Leaders.

But you'll be a better leader if, during your meetings, you think of yourself as a *facilitator*.

Here's why: *Leaders* are often looked to as the final word on any subject. They make decisions and everyone else falls in line. *Facilitators* work toward consensus, inviting input and discussion.

Leaders are the sage on the stage, imparting information to others. *Facilitators* acknowledge that anyone in the room might have valuable input, and create a safe place to share it.

Leaders talk and others listen. *Facilitators* do as much or more listening than talking.

Leaders give instructions. *Facilitators* ask questions.

Leaders direct crowds. *Facilitators* influence groups.

Leaders focus on the head. *Facilitators* focus on the heart.

Be honest: Were you walking into a small group meeting would you rather it be led by a "leader" or a "facilitator?" We're guessing facilitator, and the following tips will help you facilitate with the best of them.

Start by helping your group set discussion ground rules

Facilitators create an atmosphere conducive to civil conversation even if there's disagreement. With that in mind you suggest the following, though it's more powerful and empowering if your group reaches these conclusions on their own:

- We treat one another with respect and it shows in both tone and comments.
- We assume the best about others and their motives.
- We don't interrupt. Instead, we listen—and not just so we can counterattack.
- We honor the group's time. That means keeping comments short and on topic.
- We take people and their thoughts seriously.
- When we feel defensive, we count to ten before speaking.
- We choose to love one another.
- We each own our responsibility to maintain these ground rules.

Model what you want to see happen

If you're looking for engagement, lean forward, make eye contact, and show you're engaged yourself. Want to hear a personal story? Share one yourself. As a facilitator, it's up to you to model the attitudes and behavior you'd like to see in others.

Be a player/coach

Small group facilitators nudge the meeting through an agenda, but are also involved as participants. It's challenging to split your attention between keeping an eye on the clock and focusing on the conversation but hey—that's why you get the big bucks.

Read the room

There's no drifting off for you during meetings. As facilitator you stay aware of how people are reacting. You notice if they're checking their watches or phones. You watch body language and tone of voice to see if someone is hurting or happy, thoughtful or disengaged. And throughout each moment you're consistently praying, "God, what are you doing here? Where do you want us to steer?"

Set your own needs aside

Not completely and not forever, but during your meeting: seek to serve. Come alongside others where they're raw or hurting. If someone's voice falters as they answer a question, you'll notice. If someone becomes distant it will register with you.

And if it feels right, hit the pause button and ask a group member why he's hesitant or why her lip is trembling. You won't demand, but you'll invite. People will begin wondering if you have an empathy super-power, because you're paying attention.

Help shy people weigh in and super-talkers throttle back

Check Chapter 20 for practical ways to make this happen. For now just know it's your job as facilitator to give everyone a voice, to involve all participants.

Ask open-ended questions

See Chapter 12 for more detail, but these types of questions can't be answered with a simple "yes" or "no." They engage people and invite deep discussion. They open the door for personal stories and honest thoughts. In the hands of a skilled facilitator, they're gold.

And if you're using a curriculum that's big on closed-ended questions, take this as permission to revise them so they're open-ended. You're officially deputized.

Don't be afraid of silence

It's okay if you ask a question and nobody responds for five or ten seconds. That silence is the sound of people grappling and thinking.

Don't always be the last person to offer a comment

It's easy to fall into the rhythm of giving the last word before moving along to the next question or item on the agenda. Avoid that pattern. Why? Because you'll quickly be perceived as delivering the "correct" response before you move on.

Ask follow-up questions

Here's where you get to the really good stuff, where you find out *why* someone feels the way they feel, *how* they came to a decision. Facilitators listen closely enough that they get a sense how to peel back another layer of the discussion onion without being confrontational or coy.

Withhold judgement

When you ask what people think and they answer, it's a win! It's a win even if what they think is wrong. No, you don't turn into an angel when you die. Yes, Jesus really was without sin.

Rather than jump in to correct errors, pause and ask if everyone is on board with what was just said. Usually another group member will offer a more Biblical insight and you've been spared the role of Idea Executioner. If an error that really matters goes unchallenged you can gently suggest—as a participant—an alternative.

The truth is that, if you're creating a safe space to share, it also has to be a safe place for people to risk being wrong.

Be fearless

That lack of fear shows itself as a willingness to go the extra mile in service. It's what motivates you to take super-talkers aside to risk coaching them about how to not dominate a meeting. It's what fuels your pouring yourself into a ministry that too seldom elicits a "thank you." It's what lets you delegate not just responsibilities to other members, but also the authority to make decisions. It's what helps you strive to not create your small group in your image, but in the image of Christ.

How to Facilitate a Remote Meeting

Everything above is also part of facilitating remotely—but a remote setting makes things harder. It's harder to read the room. Harder to take note of body language. There are technical challenges that don't exist when you're in Dave and Judy's living room.

But it can be done—and it should be done.

When a pandemic shut down churches and most meetings it was tempting to put fellowship on the shelf. But never was there a time it was needed more. Never was encouragement of connection more healing and hopeful.

If you find yourself unable to meet in person, meet remotely. Here's how:

• **Pick an easy-to-use platform**

Good news: with so many people working and playing with grandkids remotely the bugs in most popular conferencing platforms are worked out. Ask what platform the majority of your group has installed (Zoom? Microsoft Teams?) and encourage everyone to download it.

• **Master the tech**

Be ready and able to coach group members about muting, unmuting, and the challenges of chat.

Not a tech whiz yourself? Get coaching from whoever does your church's media or ask a frequent user for a tutorial. YouTube will tell you what you need to know, too.

• **Manage the mess**

Rather than ask everyone to respond to a question, ask our question and then go around your screen, inviting people one at a time or in groups of three to share responses. It's not ideal, but it works.

• **Do a quick check when your meeting begins**

Is everyone visible? Unmuted? Is there a distraction (a barking dog, a thumping ceiling fan) causing problems? Address issues at the outset.

• **If possible, use timed breakout sessions**

Sending trios off for more intimate conversations in breakout rooms helps the discussion be more meaningful. You can set up the rooms and even assign participants to rooms before your meeting begins. Not sure how to do it? Ask about it when you're getting help mastering the tech.

• **Cameras on**

You need all the help you can get reading the room. Before the meeting make it clear you need everyone to be visible. No hiding.

• **Speak to the camera, not your image on screen**

It's a small thing but gives you the added bonus of appearing to make eye contact. Keep an eye on time by placing a clock where you can see it with an inconspicuous glance.

• **And ban multi-tasking**

Group members will be tempted to play a game or check emails during your meeting. Get agreement going in that won't happen. You'll need to pay close attention to one another.

CHAPTER 12

THE POWER OF QUESTIONS

*A*n enormously effective tool in your leader toolbox is a well-timed, well-presented question. Questions can loosen up your group, tighten their focus on a lesson, and move your meetings along any direction you choose.

But how do you make your questions engaging and irresistible? Try the following:

Ask open-ended questions

Questions that can't be answered with a simple "yes," "no," or a fact encourage group members to think before they respond. These questions encourage discussion, deepen understanding, and invite elaboration—all of which build relationships.

Work to fill your meeting with open-ended questions. They open up insights into what your group thinks and values.

Be clear

Avoid words that have multiple meanings or questions that include theological terms group members don't really understand. You won't get meaningful answers and people feel dumb.

Be brief

Until you've practiced asking open-ended questions it's nearly impossible to craft a clear, brief question right out of the gate. That's okay; as you prepare a lesson jot your questions down and edit them until they're ready.

Be specific

Takes a lot of brain processing power to figure out what you intend with a too-general question. "Tell me about your childhood" is too broad if you're interested in someone's faith story.

Better: "I'm wondering about how faith figured into your childhood. How did that look?"

In this example you've narrowed the topic with a statement and then followed up with a question. It's a technique worth practicing.

Be purposeful

As a facilitator you want to prompt discovery in the hearts and minds of your group. Questions can do that—but only if they're the relevant questions. Be sure every question is aiming your group where you want to go.

One question per question

Let your group deal with one thing at a time.

Here's an example of a complex question: "When people say the Bible is inspired, do you think that refers to the content of the Bible or the way the Bible was written and, if it's the latter, do you think Christians writing today can be truly inspired or simply spiritually informed?" Um, what? Complex questions require decoding—they're like hitting a wall. Keep questions direct and simple.

Don't evaluate answers—either positive or negative

This is counter-intuitive because we want to reward people who participate by offering them praise.

Resist doing that, at least verbally. Here's why: If Dewain gives an answer and you say, "Great! Super insight! Well done!" you've just guaranteed nobody else will talk. Smarty-pants Dewain has clearly given the right answer. What else is there to say?

So instead smile at Dewain and say "thank you for sharing." You've left the door open for more responses.

Create a safe environment for dissent

If you ask a question that could have multiple answers and everyone lands on one response, make it safe to have a different opinion by saying, "Thanks for sharing your thoughts. Does anyone see it differently? Does anyone have a different thought?"

Allow time for a response

When we ask question and get no answer the silence is excruciating for us. But rather than jump in and answer your own question, sweat it out for five to ten seconds. Almost always someone will break the silence with a response.

If you can see your group is confused, try rephrasing the question.

No lightbulbs turning on over the heads of your group? Invite one or two people to tell you what they're thinking, even if it's "Your question is confusing."

Still nothing? Beat a retreat—either nobody sees the relevance, nobody cares, or you've completely failed to make yourself understood. Better to move on and live to ask questions another day.

If you're looking for stories in response to your question, you go first

Group members will see what sort of response you want and have time to think about what they'll say.

Here's how that might look: "Paul was willing to risk everything for the chance to share the Gospel. I'm wondering if you've ever risked something to share it. As for me, I was at a family reunion and..."

Follow up questions are your super-power

They signal you've been listening, which is felt as caring. And they signal respect: you're communicating that the person speaking is important enough that you want to know more. Here are some comfortable ways to ask a follow-up question:

- "So you were adopted. Tell me more about that experience."
- "I'm wondering how being adopted has influenced how you look at life."
- "That moment when you discovered you were adopted must have been a before-and-after moment in your life. Tell me how you were feeling when you got the news."

Notice: None of those invitations to talk more about being adopted are actually questions—they're statements. But they'll be heard as questions and get answers.

To sum up: An open-ended question that's personal, specific, and surprising is all but guaranteed to elicit a response—and prompt a discovery-rich discussion.

Use 'em.

CHAPTER 13

GOING DEEPER

*B*efore your group can go deeper, you need to define what that means.

In a Bible study group it may mean adding Bible geography or first-century Greek to a more casual Bible study. To a *Knitting For God* group it might be tackling that Textured Fair Isle Cardigan that makes grown knitters weep.

For most groups going deeper is likely about becoming more vulnerable in your group. About deepening friendships. About growing closer to one another and to God.

But here's the thing: Relationships move at the speed of trust. If you want your group to experience deeper relationships, it comes down to trust. And you can't just demand that people trust one another.

That's not how trust works.

As the group leader, it's up to you to lead the way to greater trust. Your modeling vulnerability signals it's okay for everyone else to take a few risks. Your behavior opens the door to deeper sharing when you do the following:

Lead with integrity

If you say your group is a safe place to be honest, deliver on that promise. If you claim there's confidentiality, insist group members honor that boundary. And when you make a mistake as a leader (it happens), admit it, take responsibility, and ask for forgiveness. Say what you mean and do what you say.

Don't duck the truth

Trust grows when group members can risk telling each other the truth in love. It's a delicate balance and your group won't always get it right. But as trust grows you'll also grow in your ability to hold one another accountable. You can move past spiritual niceties to iron-sharpening-iron discipleship.

Go slow

The safest way to into the deep end of the pool is to wade in from the shallow end. True at the community pool, true in your small group.

So don't expect too much too soon; give group members time to learn to trust you and one another. And don't expect every group member to be equally ready to take a leap off the high dive at the same time.

Rick Howerton learned the hard way that getting too deep too fast can give a group the collective bends.

"I've learned the value of progressive disclosure," says Howerton. "When a group first starts meeting people aren't ready to open their hearts and share their stories. Then the leader shares something vulnerable and the group opens up a bit. As disclosures progress to more intimate places over time, the group naturally feels more comfortable. You've got to move gradually."

But when he was first a group leader, Howerton wasn't big on *gradually*.

"I opened up too quickly and instead of moving us forward I slowed us down. Group members pulled back because I was taking them to dangerous places too quickly."

Howerton's approach now: Go slow. You'll get there.

Invest in your people

Listen well and then follow up. Serve group members in practical ways and encourage them to serve one another. Pray for group members and ask them to pray for one another. When you invest in your group, your trust for your group grows. When people in your group invest in one another, the same thing happens.

Get even smaller

To increase intimacy in sharing, consider occasionally forming pairs or trios to discuss how to apply the lesson. Oftentimes, the smaller the audience, the greater the transparency. Or break the men and women into separate groups. That can invite deeper sharing, too

Consider a full-day retreat

This can be hard to pull off, but the extra hours together can bond group members together. A hike, a day in a borrowed cabin at a lake, even a day of working alongside one another—all create shared experiences and the opportunity to talk freely.

Talk about the faithfulness of God

Trust isn't just about your trusting one another; it's also about trusting God. So talk about how God has been faithful in the past and how you're trusting him to be faithful in the future. Celebrate when group members see God working in their lives.

Trust will draw your group closer to God—and he'll meet them there and walk them deeper into a friendship with himself.

CHAPTER 14

ENCOURAGING GROUP MEMBERS AND BUILDING RELATIONSHIPS

*D*o you want to make sure attendance isn't a problem with your small group? That people jot "group" on their calendars and do their best to show up every time? Then make your group a place of encouragement.

Reid Smith loves encouragement. He's worked to make it part of every small group he's organized, led, and attended since 199And if he has his way, encouragement will be a hallmark of your small group, too.

"Encouragement is so significant it's listed as a spiritual gift," says Smith. "It's so important that God tells us to encourage one another daily. It's what helps us stay faithful when life comes at us." (1 Thessalonians 5:11, Romans 12:8, Hebrews 3:13)

Which means you want your group to earn a reputation for lifting people up, to be the place group members find support as they take wobbly steps forward in their journey with Jesus.

Here are a few reasons Smith wants encouragement to become part of your group's DNA:

• **Encouragement helps your group stay faithful.** When we're battling on our own we're easily defeated. But when we face life together, urging one another to stand firm, it's hard to move us. The power of God shows up in remarkable ways when we encourage one another.

• **Encouragement propels us out of our comfort zone.** Jesus often asks us to say and do things that feel too hard to say and do. Forgiving others, giving testimony, confessing sins—none are easy. But when others encourage us and hold us accountable, we're emboldened to do those and more.

• **Encouragement helps us feel loved.** If you've ever faced something hard and then felt a hand squeeze your shoulder, you know how it feels to be encouraged...and loved. Make your group a place that happens often.

• **Encouragement reminds us: We're in this together.** The history of the early church is one of encouragement. Jesus encouraged his disciples. The disciples encouraged one another. Missionaries encouraged the unsaved. Then and now, encouragement is part of the mission of the church—and your small group.

But how do you effectively encourage group members? And how do you turn your small group into a community of encouragers?

"Encouragement is contagious," says Smith. "The way to infuse your group with encouragement is to be encouraging yourself." So feel free to talk about encouragement but know this: It won't become a part of your group culture until you model it yourself.

Courtesy of Smith (and others), here's how to do that:

• **Pay attention.** When others speak lean forward, make eye contact, and nod at appropriate times to show you're taking in what's being shared. Put away your phone so there are no distractions. It's encouraging to be seen, heard, and valued.

• **Affirm the good you see in group members.** Let people know when you see them reflecting Jesus' love, or serving selflessly. It's encouraging to know God is using you; help group members experience that encouragement and appreciate the positive impact they're having on others.

• **Tell your group what God says about them.** They're his sons and daughters. New creations. Seen, known, loved, and saved. "Be like a mirror holding up God's truth about your group where they can see it," says Smith. Little is more encouraging than seeing yourself as God sees you.

- **Remind your group: Jesus is present.** Where two or more of Jesus' people are gathered, he's there too. It's encouraging to know that Jesus is aware of your group and what you're doing together. Celebrate and own that truth.

- **Meet expectantly.** When Jesus is present the power to impact lives is present, too. Expect growth and transformation and, when you see it, call it out.

- **Focus on what's excellent and praiseworthy.** That's not to say you duck hard issues or messy situations. But look for what God is doing in those moments, refusing to give in to despair. Philippians 4:8 isn't permission to ignore what's unjust or broken; it's encouragement to lean into the Lord.

- **Be available.** "Be one of those 2 a.m. friends," says Smith. "See that everyone has your number and knows they can call you day or night. Most people will never make that call, but knowing they could is an encouragement. They know they're not alone."

- **Connect.** Make an encouraging phone call. Send an affirming note in the mail. Tap out an appreciative text. "Let people know you're thinking about them and you believe in them," says Smith.

- **Challenge people to use their gifts.** "Lots of believers don't understand that they're gifted and need to use those gifts," says Smith. "It matters when you say to someone, 'I see something in you. I see God has blessed you so you can bless others.' That challenge is encouragement to find new ways to exercise God-given gifts."

- **Get practical.** When group members reveal needs, ask God how you can help meet them. Note: You can't meet every need, nor should you try. But at minimum you can circle back to find out how things are going.

- **Remember birthdays and anniversaries.** Gather that information when your group first launches and when key dates arrive pause to celebrate. One small group lights a candle on a birthday cupcake and then slices the cupcake into ten or twelve pieces for distribution. Nothing bonds a group like celebrating while making a mess!

- **Remember the names of group members' children.** When the group leader asks about your kids by name, that signals you're more than just one more person who comes to group.

- **Share a task.** Spend a Saturday morning assisting someone with a chore. You'll have time to talk as you weed that garden together or paint that fence.

- **Be a no-put down zone.** It's easy to get a cheap laugh by pointing out a flaw in someone's thinking or behavior—but it's far from encouraging. Don't let this sort of humor find a home in your group. If you've got someone who likes to needle others, take that person aside and have a chat.

- **Switch pews.** We tend to sit in the same place at church services. Instead, look for a small group member and ask if you can sit with him or her. That helps shift your relationship from leader/group member to friend/friend. Encouraging!

- **Pray for people in your group—and let them know.** When you pray for members of your group, you come to love them more sincerely. You see more to appreciate and affirm, more to encourage.

  Should a prayer need arise during group meetings, don't wait to pray. Ask group members to gather around the person who shared the need, lay reassuring hands on that person's shoulders, and pray on the spot. That support is deeply encouraging.

- **Keep your encouragement tank full, too.** In time, as your group becomes a community of encouragers, you'll be encouraged there, too. But until then, seek out other leaders who can support and encourage you in your role as a small group leader...and as someone growing in Christ.

CHAPTER 15

WHAT TO DO WHEN PEOPLE DISAPPEAR

*W*hen someone stops coming to your group and there's no apparent reason—a move, job change, or shift in family status, you face a decision: Do you say something, or not? You do.

Jesus made a point of checking on stray sheep (Matthew 18:12-14), and as a leader, tracking down strays is your job, too.

"The goal isn't to get them back in your group at all costs," says Carlos, a small group leader in Colorado. "Your goal is to make sure they're in fellowship somewhere and there are no broken relationships to address."

So follow up, but do so respectfully. If possible, find out the reason for leaving. Was it unmet expectations? Your group just wasn't a fit? Anything said or done that created problems? What can you learn that will help you be a better leader?

You're essentially conducting an exit interview and, if you suspect tension between you and the person who left might be an issue, you're probably not the person to explore the reasons for departure.

Better: Ask your Assistant Group Leader to have the conversation and brief you about what's said.

The person leaving may be more transparent if you're not sitting in the room. This isn't ducking your responsibility to resolve differences; if your name comes up as a reason for breaking with the group you can follow up to discuss it.

If there's nothing for you to resolve, call to thank the person who's leaving for their involvement, bless them as they go, and offer to help them find a small group that will meet their needs. At minimum you can tell the person coordinating your church's small groups what happened so the coordinator can provide information about other groups.

You can keep your focus on those other 99 sheep who need your attention.

CHAPTER 16

PRAYING AS A GROUP

When your group prays together, you're reminding group members God is with you. You're inviting group members to experience the power of prayer, to bask in God's presence, and to invite God to speak into their lives.

But it's possible some of your group might be uncomfortable praying aloud. And some of your group might pray only occasionally or not at all.

To address the first issue, don't insist anyone in your group pray aloud. Avoid situations like going around the circle asking everyone to pray in turn.

And the second issue? Use the following approaches to introduce your group to prayer that's engaging, intimate, and dynamic.

Create prayer partners

Form pairs or trios in your group and have smaller groups huddle to pray together. It's less intimidating than praying in front of the whole group, and encourages more transparent sharing. Ask that partners pray for each other rather than themselves.

Embrace silent prayer

You can list prayer concerns one by one and pause after each to let group members silently pray for them. With no one but God listening, group members can pray as honestly as they'd like.

Pray a Psalm together

Take turns reading passages (but be careful: some people also struggle with reading aloud), pausing after each phrase so your group can prayerfully consider the passages.

Ask that everyone pray for the person on their left

Silently, or aloud, have group members pray for the person next to them.

Take a knee

Ask everyone to assume a posture that honors God. People may choose to kneel, bow, or stand; some might raise their hands. Ask the group to then pray silently or invite volunteers to pray aloud.

Include body movement in prayer

Something as simple as praying with cupped hands, standing and facing away from the circle, or placing a hand on the shoulder of a partner can take prayer to a deeper level.

Pray with eyes open, looking at other members of the group

Try this: pray for others while looking at them and letting them lock eyes with you. There's a greater connection, a stronger intimacy.

Pray the Lord's Prayer together

As group members listen, pray through Matthew 6:9-1Don't offer commentary; simply let group members experience the prayer as it unfolds. Using an unusual translation of scripture may help group members focus more on the content of what Jesus prayed.

Listen. Just listen

Rather than speaking, ask group members to invite God to speak to them and then have two minutes of silence. You can extend the time of silence as your group becomes accustomed to listening prayer. Ask the group to share what—if anything—they heard.

Leave the room for a prayer walk

If you're meeting in a neighborhood, walk out the door and down the block. Pause to pray for people who live in each residence you pass.

Switch up the prayer time in your group

There's no rule it has to happen at the end of your meeting time. How about starting with prayer, or praying toward the middle of your meeting?

Invite group members to suggest issues close to their hearts

Pray for those in poverty, for government leaders, or for war-torn parts of the globe. Focus on one heart-felt issue per meeting.

Offer a praise-only prayer

Invite volunteers to offer prayers aloud that focus on praise-worthy attributes of God, or prayers that are focused on thanks for who he is and what he's done. No requests!

Pass around something to taste

Give each person a pinch of salt to taste before praying for people who are thirsty for clean water. Have people taste lemon slices to prompt prayers for those experiencing bitter times. Let the senses of taste or smell add immediacy to your prayer time.

Involve sight, too

Print a picture. Show a brief video. Hang a map on the wall or light a candle. Take advantage of the gift of sight to prompt prayers.

Ask God what you should pray about

We often start talking just to fill space. Instead, ask group members to sit quietly for several minutes, silencing their minds, inviting God to give them a word, song, snippet of scripture, or an image to direct their prayers. After the experience ask for volunteers to share what happened during the time of silence.

If you have group members who aren't open to new ways to pray, position new approaches as an experiment, something you'll try once just to see how it goes. If it goes well you might do it again. But if it doesn't connect with your group, it will never again show up in the agenda.

Even people who don't like change are often open to experiments.

CHAPTER 17

WORSHIPPING AS A GROUP

*W*hen it comes to small group worship, John Cutshall says it's all in how you define the word "worship." As both a pastor and worship leader, John's aware most churches use the word as shorthand for "stand and sing."

Which is far from the best definition of "worship." "Worship is showing reverence to God," says John. "Singing is one way but hardly the only way. And it may not necessarily be the best way in a small group."

John is always up for pulling out his guitar to lead singing, but he knows what you're about to discover: not everyone is a fan.

"I'm self-conscious about my voice so I lip synch or mumble during worship songs at church," says Mike, a small group member. "On Sunday mornings no one can tell. But if at our next small group meeting I'm told to sing, well, I'm pretty much out of there."

Nudging Mike out of his comfort zone isn't a bad thing, but if it sends him bolting for the door maybe singing isn't the way to go.

John has been in groups where singing was part of the shared experience, and groups where it wasn't. And his advice to you as a leader is to check with the group before making singing a thing. "Find out if they're comfortable with it," says John.

If your group *is* up for choruses, you'll still need to adjust your expectations. "When you're leading singing with a hundred people joining you, you expect a certain involvement and volume.

That won't be there in a small group."

One suggestion from John if you want to give singing a try: "Tell your group they can sing if they want to, but it's fine if they just close their eyes and focus on the lyrics, allowing those words to touch their hearts. It takes pressure off the non-singers."

Want to worship without singing? Here are a few ways for that to happen:

- **Read the names of Jesus found in scripture**. A partial list is at the end of this chapter. Rather than going through all the names at one time, select a few (three to six) to focus on at a time. Pause between the names as you read them aloud and ask group members to reflect on what those names say about Jesus.

  Tip: Note on the list which ones you have done to help you in selecting a different batch for the next time.
- **Be intentionally thankful.** Thank God for the things you normally overlook: fresh water, air in your lungs, the health of your teeth or elbows. John's favorite suggestion came from a child: "I'm thankful that the holes in my nose are on the bottom instead of the top because if it was the other way when it rained I could drown."
- **Write a praise**. The act of writing requires intentionally. Write and then read aloud why you find God worthy of honor.
- **Raise your hands**. Part of praise is surrender to God. Actively do so.
- **Pray with your eyes open**. Thank God for the things—and people—you see.
- **Serve one another**. We praise God when we do as he asks and we reflect his values. Serving one another for the right reasons praises God.
- **Read scripture passages**. Pick those that describe the greatness and glory of God. The Psalms are a great place to start.

• **Listen to a worship song**. Don't sing it. Instead, let the singers lead you into an attitude of praise and adoration. Linger there and respond to the experience. Let worship flow out of your group members as they focus on God.

• **And a bonus**: Whatever your group suggests that you wouldn't think of. It's very possible one or more group members is more attune to worship than you are. Invite ideas and leadership from group members who can draw your group into the throne room of God.

Names of Jesus:

The Alpha and Omega (Rev. 1:8; 22:13)
Immanuel (Matt 1:22-23)
King of kings and Lord of lords (1 Tim 6:15)
Light of the World (John 9:5)
Morning Star (Rev 22:16)
Righteous One (Acts 7:52)
Prince of Peace (Isaiah 9:6)
Wonderful Counselor (Isaiah 9:6)
Lamb of God (John 1:29)
Savior (Eph 5:23)
Good Shepherd (John 10:11, 14)
The Way (John 14:6)
Great High Priest (Heb 4:14-16)
Cornerstone (Eph 2:20)
Bread of Life (John 6:35; 6:48)
Lord of Glory (1 Cor 2:8)
Messiah (Matt 1:1)
Teacher (John 3:2)
The Truth (John 14:6)
Hope of the World (Luke 2:25-35)

CHAPTER 18

REACHING OUT AS A GROUP

*P*lanning an outreach or service project can be as easy or complicated as you want. Some groups pick a Saturday morning and fan out to pick up trash in a neighborhood. Others coordinate vacation weeks and take mission trips together.

If your group is new it's the perfect time to let your group decide what sort of outreach and service to embrace.

Start by grappling as a group with these questions:

Who are we?

God has equipped your group to serve, but how? Ask your group what skills, interests, and gifts they bring to the table. What are their physical limitations? Time constraints? Find out what they do for a living, knowing some of them won't want to serve doing the same thing they do all week.

Find out who you are and what you care about and you'll have some sense of what an effective, rewarding service project might be.

What's our church already doing?

There may be projects in which your group members are already involved. If that's the case perhaps you can try doing one of them as a group.

Do we want to do a one-off project or commit longer term?

Carter Moss suggests your small group consider investing deeply in one project so you'll make a significant impact.

"Instead of going to the homeless shelter this week and doing a beach clean-up next week, form a partnership and spend time serving with that partner," he says. "Maybe there's a neighborhood soccer league needing help. Maybe you all have a heart for girls who've been trafficked. See if your group will adopt a cause connected to a shared passion.

"If your group is just getting started, try a few different things," says Moss. "See what speaks to you and then pray about what your service focus might be."

And if you're wanting to combine service with evangelism, Moss suggests this: throw a party.

"Host a barbeque and have group members invite non-Christian friends," says Moss. "Our church resources those kinds of events. We tell groups to stop by the church and borrow tables, chairs, and canopies. We say to take the popcorn machine anytime they want it."

Whether your group serves in a series of one-time events or strikes up a partnership, either option beats doing nothing at all.

How long will we commit to serve?

From the start have a date when your service project ends. That way people you serve will have realistic expectations and so will your group. When the time to move on arrives, your group can celebrate a job well done.

How can everyone be involved?

If you want everyone to participate, give everyone a job.

Frank's bad back won't let him help paint a school classroom, but he can show up to cheer on the troops and give them backrubs. Cheri can't give blood at the church blood drive you're organizing, but she can bake cookies for donors.

When you meet after the outreach event to debrief, make sure everyone has a story to share.

How will this activity clearly share Christ?

Your group's goal isn't to stay busy. It's to advance the Kingdom both within and beyond your group members. Sort out up front how an outreach effort will share Christ. If the project is a fit—go for it.

Work through these questions with your group and you'll see a plan come into focus. If it doesn't, read through the following list and see which outreach opportunities spark interest or suggest even better ideas:

- Organize a church blood drive
- Provide childcare during a parents-night out
- Paint the church nursery
- Visit a nursing home and visit with residents who don't get many visitors
- Shop for shut-ins
- Host a Halloween alternative event
- Organize and staff a night of prayer at your church building
- Call on people who've recently visited your church
- Set up a community garden
- Organize an art show
- Sponsor a sidewalk chalk event
- Show up at youth group with enough snacks to feed an army
- Send care packages to college students
- Appreciate your pastor with a serenade and a gift card
- Bless a missionary with a shipment of cards and goodies
- Got skills? Bless a single mom with auto repair or handyman tasks

- Tutor students
- Host a family movie night at the church...and serve popcorn
- Go Christmas caroling (extra points of it's in August)
- Organize a fundraiser for a worthy charity
- Help at a homeless shelter or soup kitchen
- Call a local non-profit and ask how they could use you for a day
- Partner with a respite care facility
- Hand out water at a community event
- Tell Habitat for Humanity you're ready to swing some hammers
- Write to men and women serving in the military or at VA hospitals
- Three words: free car wash
- Two words: mow lawns
- One word: Par-tay!

CHAPTER 19

HOW TO PICK A SMALL GROUP STUDY

*J*f you're leading a sermon-review group, the decision about what biblical content to use has been made for you. And affiliation groups seldom need much content at all.

But other kinds of small groups will likely require curriculum, typically an eight- to twelve-week series of lessons from a publisher or well-known church leader. Some are topical (how to be a better disciple, how to find peace) and others are straight Bible studies. Both, if from reputable sources, can be theologically sound and engaging.

As group leader, you'll want to narrow down options available to your group. You also need to decide: Will you choose the curriculum or put it to a vote?

The upside of presenting options for a vote is buy-in. Adults in small groups like to have a voice about how they'll spend the next few months, and choosing a topic is no exception.

The upside of you making a decision yourself is that you can pick a curriculum you're comfortable leading...though you may find nobody else is interested.

Or select a middle-ground: seek input from group members regarding topics and then search for a suitable curriculum to bring back for a vote.

Either way, it's helpful to have a yardstick by which to measure curriculums. There are literally hundreds of options, and you'll be ahead if you narrow down choices by asking these 15 questions:

What's the spiritual maturity and biblical literacy of your group?

Is your group cracking open their Bibles for the first time? Do you have dedicated students of the Bible who've mastered the basics? Is there a mix?

You want to find lessons that are accessible to everyone in the group. If you have a wide range of spiritual maturity and Biblical literacy to address, remember well-written application questions make any lesson relevant.

Are there pressing needs that must be addressed?

If your community has just experienced a school shooting, your group may need to explore how to respond to issues related to the shooting before they're ready to focus on anything else. Forgiveness, the sovereignty of God, grace—those topics may be far more meaningful than a broader study.

How long do you meet? And for what duration?

If your meetings are for forty-five minutes and you allot fifteen for the lesson, pick a curriculum that doesn't deliver thirty minutes of material. Or adapt lessons to turn each into a two-parter. Committing to a series of 12 lessons gives you flexibility to try something new in three months or so. You aren't locked in for a year.

What's the source of the curriculum?

Not every good curriculum comes from reputable Christian publishers, but buying from a source that's been carefully written, edited, and theologically vetted is generally a good idea.

Does the curriculum fit your focus?

If you're aiming for creating a community of care, is discussion valued? If you're after Biblical depth, do you see it in the lessons?

How is the Bible handled in the curriculum?

Be sure it's respected as God's Word rather than just one more moral book. Reading a few lessons will surface how the Bible is regarded. Also see how much scripture is in each lesson, and whether passages are explored deeply.

What's the theology?

Because publishers want to reach a wide audience, lessons generally focus on what different denominations have in common. But check to see if a denominational publisher gives an outsized emphasis to their unique theological slant.

Can you afford the curriculum?

If each group member needs a $25 book, is that affordable? Can you or your church cover the cost? Committing to that curriculum is committing to making sure every member has a book.

Are there application opportunities?

If you're hoping to see discipleship deepen and accountability happen, lessons need to be both relevant and applicable. How is application handled in the lessons?

Is the curriculum boring?

Be honest: If you're bored reading sample lessons, how bored will your group be as you present them? And they won't be blaming the lesson material.

Can studies be led by other group members?

If so—if the lessons are clear and well-organized—you have the opportunity to encourage others to develop their leadership skills.

Does the material require wi-fi access or ancillary materials?

Some curriculum assumes you can stream video segments while other curricula requires additional purchases.

Are questions open-ended, respectful, and thought-provoking?

If questions are just reciting the facts that were presented, move on. You need engaging questions that will spark deep conversation. Some should be surprising, all should be personal and specific.

Will you find a study that checks off every item on the list above? Probably not, but you *can* find a study that delivers those you care most about.

Oh, and something to keep in mind: if you pick a curriculum that doesn't include something you think essential, you'll likely be revising the lessons to include it.

CHAPTER 20

IN CASE OF EMERGENCY—TIPS FOR ADDRESSING CHALLENGES

A group member's house burns down. A marriage blows up. There's a sudden sickness, church scandal, or the suicide of a friend.

Your group members may experience any of a thousand different problems, and those problems have this in common: They're elephants in the room demanding your attention.

It's the height of insensitivity to ignore a group member's pain. No lesson you planned is more important than responding to an urgent need staring you in the face.

So don't ignore the elephants. Not the ones who thunder in to disrupt your meetings or the ones who quietly edge their way into the room.

"Some problems that impact your group are obvious," says Colorado small group leader Carlos. "But others happen slowly. Spotty attendance or people looking bored may not feel like a problem, but in time they'll kill your group. View anything hurting your people or your group as needing attention—now."

There's no one-size-fits-all solution to small group problems, but you won't go wrong clicking through the following checklist...

Pray

Ask God how he'd have you respond to the issue in front of you. You probably can't fix it; what role do you have in supporting the person who's hurting?

Pray and, if it doesn't cross confidentiality lines, ask others to pray as well.

Seek counsel

Who can you call at midnight to help you sort out what to do? As a small group leader you need that phone number. It may be your small group coordinator, your pastor, or a level-headed friend, but *have that number*. And don't use it until you need it.

Turn to scripture

The Bible says nothing about losing a job to a corporate takeover, but plenty about trusting God in trying times. Share encouragement from God's Word with hurting people who are ready to hear it, but don't forget to give a hug, too.

Act (and act quickly)

Make your way to the hospital waiting room. Call to let someone know you care. You may not have been asked for help, but that doesn't mean you can't offer it.

Report and/or refer

If you're out of your depth (someone's having a manic episode or there's self-harm revealed) let someone better equipped handle the situation. Your best assistance may be finding qualified help and assisting the hurting person to make contact. If in your judgment someone is at present risk of harming either themselves or others, getting immediate help supersedes your commitment to confidentiality.

The following are problems you may encounter during your time as a small group leader. Most deal with the group itself because, while catastrophic emergencies are rare, you can count on hitting snags when it comes to your group functioning smoothly.

You've got an especially needy person

Pray with and for this person either before or after each meeting. That keeps this person from dominating the meeting and still provides support. Consider finding another group member who'll make contact between meetings for prayer.

You've got an arguer

Point back to your covenant, especially the part about respect. Stress this isn't the place for vigorous debate or "devil's advocate" behavior. If your arguer has a specific agenda (politics come to mind) make clear the issue isn't always on the menu for discussion. If the arguer launches into a monologue during a meeting, interrupt and direct a question to someone else.

You've got a fight on your hands

Small group members don't always get along. Bring the combatants together and mediate, aiming for forgiveness and reconciliation. Solicit help from a third party if necessary. Just don't pretend nothing is happening.

You've got a talker

You can moderate a member's tendency to hold the floor by framing your questions this way: "In two or three sentences, how would you respond to this..."

Also, sit next to the talker. You can clear your throat, place a hand on the person's shoulder, or make eye contact as you transition to another person. And speak privately with the talker to address the issue. Avoid embarrassing anyone in the group meeting.

Your group wanders into the weeds

"I was with a group that had a couple knowledgeable Bible students," remembers Carlos. "They'd hijack the lesson by quoting and explaining passages that sent us off in new directions. They ended up talking to each other and the rest of us were an audience."

Carlos fixed the problem by clearly stating what the lesson was about right up front. "I eliminated end runs," he says. "When they got off-course I had permission to reign them in."

Someone reveals an addiction, adultery, or other serious problem

Unless you have credentials and expertise, this is the time to refer and refer quickly. Give the hurting individual all the support you can, but help them find appropriate, perhaps professional, help. Be aware the hurting person may not want your help other than as a listening ear; if that's the case, let it be enough.

But keep praying.

CHAPTER 21

ONE ANOTHERING

*G*etting people to your small group is one thing. Getting them to stick is another.

"Our Sunday night Bible study was wide open," remembers Nick of a small group he led in his Cincinnati home. "The first month anywhere from six to eight people showed up. They were especially generous and caring people. I loved getting together with them."

The next month the number of regulars grew to a dozen.

At the six-month mark Nick could count on a minimum of thirty people squeezing into his living and dining rooms. "People came, connected, and just never left," says Nick.

Nick's church wanted to understand Nick's secret sauce. Other groups struggled to keep members so a couple church leaders stopped by and quickly figured out the glue that held Nick's group together.

"It was how people treated each other," says Nick. "There was a culture of connectivity and service. What's strange is I didn't really have anything to do with it. A couple people in the group took it on themselves to welcome visitors and find out if someone was moving and needed help, or was sick and could use casseroles. They organized dinners and coffee dates. I just sat back and watched it happen."

Without ever intending for it to happen, Nick had in place the single best retention tool for small groups: One-Anothering. It's what transforms a collection of individuals into a cohesive group. It's what turns a commitment into a community.

Among other "one anothering" passages in scripture are those that follow. Read one or two to your group the first dozen times you meet and ask, "What would it look like if this described our relationships? What would we be saying or doing?"

Discuss it...and then look for opportunities to do it.

Become the place people look out for and love one another.

- Be at peace with each other. (Mark 9:50)
- Love one another. (John 15:17)
- Be devoted to one another in brotherly love. (Romans 12:10)
- Honor one another above yourselves. (Romans 12:10)
- Stop passing judgment on one another. (Romans 14:13)
- Accept one another, then, just as Christ accepted you. (Romans 15:7)
- Have equal concern for each other. (1 Corinthians 12:25)
- Serve one another in love. (Galatians 5:13)
- Carry each other's burdens. (Galatians 6:2)
- Be patient, bearing with one another in love. (Ephesians 4:2)
- Be kind and compassionate to one another. (Ephesians 4:32)
- Forgive whatever grievances you may have against one another. (Colossians 3:13)
- Admonish one another. (Colossians 3:16)
- Encourage each other. (1 Thessalonians 4:18)
- Build each other up. (1 Thessalonians 5:11)
- Spur one another on toward love and good deeds. (Hebrews 10:24)
- Confess your sins to each other. (James 5:16)
- Pray for each other. (James 5:16)

- Each one should use whatever gift he has received to serve others. (1 Peter 4:10)
- Clothe yourselves with humility toward one another (1 Peter 5:5)

And so you know, there's one specific "one another" that outside of its cultural context you should probably avoid: "Greet one another with a holy kiss" (Romans 16:16).

CHAPTER 22

THE CHALLENGE OF CHILDCARE

*E*ven if you don't have young children, someone in your group might. Or—and this is likelier—someone who would gladly join your group won't do so because there's no immediate childcare solution.

Someone like Cherie.

"My husband and I moved across the country so he could take his dream job," she says. "We joined a church and wanted to be in a small group again, but money was tight and we couldn't afford a weekly Sunday night babysitter.

"So for the first time in our marriage we weren't in a group. And it was a time we really needed the support and friendships that come with being in a small group."

The small groups at Cherie's church had reached the conclusion that the best way to address childcare for small groups was to simply *not* address it. None of the congregation's small groups provided any options for childcare.

You can choose to simply not address childcare, too, but consider these alternatives that may open up your group to people who want to join your group.

Arrange on-site childcare parents can use on a pay-per-child basis

Some groups hire a babysitter/childcare worker who cares for kids in one room while parents meet in another part of the house or church building.

The upside: Parents don't have to scramble to find babysitters. Carefully vetted caregivers are already recruited. Some groups hire teenagers from the youth group, others look beyond the church walls. Either way, screening and adult supervision is vital.

The challenge: You might recruit a childcare worker who arrives only to find none of the paying parents show up that week. Consider asking your group (or small group ministry) to contribute money so there's a minimum payment your worker can count on even if no children are present.

Have parents take turns providing childcare

Let parents rotate heading to the basement with the kids for the hour. And not just parents: Give any adult in your group who loves kids the chance to serve. Spry grandparents, single adults, couples who don't yet have kids but are dipping a toe in the parenthood pool—they can all take a turn.

The upside: There's little or no expense. And if you invite kids back while you pray together, kids get to see their parents praying. That's powerful.

The challenge: For some parents, small group is their adult-only date for the week. If that's the case, they may still choose to hire their own babysitters so their kids stay home.

Meet where childcare is provided

There's something intimate about meeting in a home, but if you and a few other groups choose to meet at the same time at your church building you've got great facilities to provide childcare. Ask the children's ministry to provide a volunteer to care for kids.

The upside: If your church is providing care, you have a qualified caregiver and great facilities. And with more kids in attendance, there's an opportunity for more varied activities and for more friendships to form.

The challenge: If you're using the facilities you need to clean up and bring your own supplies. Ask your children's pastor to lay out some ground rules and abide by them.

Ask another group to cover for you (and do the same for them)

Ask another group to provide supervision for your kids when you meet if you'll do the same for them when they meet. You send a vetted volunteer to them on Thursday and they provide one on Sunday.

The upside: No adult has to leave your meeting to care for the kids, and the same is true for your partner group. Plus, there's no out-of-pocket expense other than providing snacks for kids and any resource materials that might be needed.

The challenge: Coordination is required, especially if you move your meetings from one house to another.

Cherie and her husband eventually returned to a small group, though not until their oldest child was capable of caring for his little sister while Cherie and her husband were away at group.

"I'd have given a lot to have access to a small group when we needed it most," Cherie says. "I've got to believe other people feel the same way right now."

Talk with your Small Group Director to find out what childcare options have been tried in the past. What's worked, what hasn't worked, and what might you try?

If you do choose to provide some sort of childcare, include that information in any advertising you do for your group. Also, let people you invite know. Be clear if there's a cost, and also describe what vetting will be done with childcare providers.

CHAPTER 23

BONUS SMALL GROUP LEADER TIPS

*B*y our count you've already received 447 great tips and 4 so-so ones, but there's always room for a few more! (The good ones, that is.)

Here's a quick jog through what else our veteran leaders want to make sure you know as you start your small group ministry:

- If you have non-believers attending, don't offend them by assuming everyone has a Christian worldview. Expect to be challenged when you make faith-related claims.

- Ask ahead if you want someone to share his or her faith story. Some people aren't sure what to say.

- Ask people to turn off or silence their cell phones and to not check for messages during your meeting. But don't be rigid about it—parents may need to be available to kids or babysitters.

- Double-check the bathroom. Make sure everything is spotless and there's an extra roll of toilet tissue visible.

- Thank people for coming. Their presence is a gift.

- As soon as people leave, take notes on what happened—especially prayer requests.

- Breath mints.

- Don't play favorites. You'll have them, but no one should be able to tell.

- If you're married, don't let your group time impinge on your spouse time.
- Be yourself. God called you to lead your group, not your favorite pastor.
- Connect with another small group leader and pinky swear to support each other.
- Don't assume anyone remembers anything, including you. Confirm meeting dates and times.
- Check allergies and gluten tolerance before buying snacks.
- Tell people if they're showing up straight from work, feel free to bring dinner to eat during your meeting. No, they don't have to bring enough for everyone.
- Encourage small group members to also attend church services. Your small group isn't a substitute.
- If something isn't working, it's okay to toss it and try something new. A study. A format. A meeting night.
- It's okay if you don't have all the answers.
- (Did we mention breath mints?)

CHAPTER 24
MEETING CHECKLISTS

*H*ere are some checklists that may be helpful as reminders ahead of your small group meeting.

A week before your meeting:
- ☐ Confirm meeting time and location with group
- ☐ Write agenda
- ☐ Review content lesson, if any
- ☐ Select opener and closer
- ☐ Pray

A few days before your meeting:
- ☐ Confirm refreshments
- ☐ Confirm meeting space
- ☐ Quick reminder text or email to group
- ☐ Review agenda
- ☐ Pray

Twenty minutes before anyone else arrives:
- ☐ Review lesson content
- ☐ Set phone to vibrate
- ☐ Arrange seats in a circle
- ☐ Set out refreshments
- ☐ Check lighting and temperature
- ☐ Turn on music

- ☐ Set out name tags and pens
- ☐ Remove pets from meeting area
- ☐ Place discrete clock
- ☐ Pray

During your meeting:
- ☐ Greet people warmly
- ☐ Facilitate meeting
- ☐ Focus on building relationships
- ☐ Follow agenda as the Lord leads
- ☐ Discuss group covenant
- ☐ Pray

After your meeting:
- ☐ Evaluate meeting
- ☐ Thank those who attended
- ☐ Plan next meeting
- ☐ Pray

CHAPTER 25

SAMPLE SMALL GROUP JOB DESCRIPTIONS

*C*hapter 5 provided a sample job description for a small group leader. Following are some additional samples related to jobs that are sometimes divided up among group members. Each group is unique and some of these may not be applicable to your group or the way your church organizes or divides duties among groups. Pick and choose as you like what is helpful to you and your group.

Assistant Group Leader Job Description
Role:

To assist the Small Group Leader in leading and facilitating a group in such a way it promotes healthy relationships, deepens faith in God, and equips and empowers group members for ministry.

Responsible to:

Small Group Leader

Prerequisites:

1. Must be an active member of First Church
2. Attend small group leadership orientation and other team meetings
3. Affirm First Church's Statement of Beliefs
4. Demonstrate a desire to use spiritual gifts in a small group leadership setting
5. Share and support the vision of First Church to disciple others

6. Have an ability to communicate clearly and well
7. Be teachable

Length of Commitment:
One year, renewable at 11 months

Responsibilities:
1. In conjunction with the Small Group Leader, advertise the group and invite potential participants.
2. Attend all group meetings unless unavoidable circumstances prevent attendance.
3. As directed by the Small Group Leader, prepare and lead sharing, prayer, Bible content, and application at meetings.
4. Assist with organizing at least two small group service projects per year.
5. Pray for each group member daily
6. Embrace responsibility for nurturing relationships within the group.
7. Foster a sense of outreach that results in group members extending invitations to adults outside the church to join the group.
8. Meet monthly with the Small Group Leader (by phone or in person)

Host Job Description
Role:
Provide a comfortable, inviting environment for small group meetings, either in a home or other setting.

Responsible to:
Small Group Leader

Prerequisites:
1. Must be an active member of First Church
2. Affirm First Church's Statement of Beliefs
3. Share and support the vision of First Church to disciple others
4. Have a spiritual gift or sincere interest in hospitality
5. Have an ability to communicate clearly and well
6. Be teachable

Length of Commitment:
One year, renewable at 11 months

Responsibilities:
1. Provide a comfortable, inviting environment for group meetings.
2. Assure that any needed technology is present and working.
3. Arrange suitable seating, preferably in a circle.
4. Set up refreshments before the meeting time.
5. Warmly greet attendees by name as they arrive.
6. Introduce visitors to group members.
7. Wait until group participants have left to clean up and rearrange furniture.
8. Connect monthly with the Small Group Leader by phone or in person.
9. Pray for the group.

Food Coordinator Job Description
Role:
Ensure a variety of simple snacks for each group meeting, either by providing them or coordinating with other group members to provide them.

Responsible to:
Small Group Leader

Prerequisites:
1. Have a spiritual gift or sincere interest in hospitality
2. Have an ability to communicate clearly and well
3. Be teachable

Length of Commitment:
One year, renewable at 11 months

Responsibilities:
1. Provide a variety of simple snacks for each group meeting, being sensitive to dietary restrictions and health preferences of group members.
2. Arrive early enough to assist the host in putting out snacks.
3. Connect monthly with the Small Group Leader by phone or in person.
4. Pray for the group.

Outreach Coordinator Job Description
Role:
In conjunction with the Small Group Leader, organize outreach/service events designed to build group cohesiveness, serve the community, and engage potential new group members.

Responsible to:
Small Group Leader

Prerequisites:
1. Have a spiritual gift or sincere interest in service
2. Have an ability to communicate clearly and well
3. Be teachable

Length of Commitment:
One year, renewable at 11 months

Responsibilities:
1. Organize and facilitate two (or more—consult with the Small Group Leader) outreach/service events in which group members will participate.
2. Solicit service ideas from the group and provide ideas as well; work with the group to come to a consensus on which activities to pursue.
3. Accept responsibility for coordinating event details and making arrangements.
4. Connect monthly with the Small Group Leader by phone or in person.
5. Pray for the group.

In-reach Coordinator Job Description
Role:
When needs arise within the group for meal delivery or other one-another acts of service, this person will initiate and coordinate providing practical assistance and encouragement by contacting and organizing group members. This individual will also see that birthdays and anniversaries are noted and celebrated.

Responsible to:
Small Group Leader

Prerequisites:
1. Have a spiritual gift or sincere interest in service
2. Be comfortable managing details and calendars
3. Have an ability to communicate clearly and well
4. Be teachable

Length of Commitment:
One year, renewable at 11 months

Responsibilities:
1. As needed, organize meal deliveries and other one-another acts of service for group members.
2. Serve as a point of contact for group members when events arise that might call for practical, caring help from other group members.
3. Connect monthly and as needed with the Small Group Leader by phone or in person.
4. Pray for the group.

CHAPTER 26

DISCUSSION QUESTIONS

*Y*ou'll deepen your skills as you discuss the following questions with other small group leaders.

Section 1 Questions

After introducing yourselves, talk about this:

- What's one of the best experiences you've had in a small group? What's an experience you don't remember fondly?
- Which of the "one anothering" encouragements listed in Chapter 1 do you think is top-of-the-list important to see in your small group? Why that one?
- As you lead (or think about leading) a small group, what if anything causes you concern?

Section 2 Questions

- Balancing tasks and people is tough. Given your natural inclinations, which do you think you tend to favor: finishing tasks or connecting with people? What's an example from your life (group, work, or home) that supports that conclusion?
- Having a "shepherd's heart" is crucial for small group leaders. Tell a story about someone whose "shepherd's heart" has helped you. Who was

the shepherd and what happened? What lessons about shepherding can you learn and apply to shepherding your small group?

- How comfortable are you recruiting members for your small group? What helps you invite others and what gets in your way?

Section 3 Questions

- Without identifying the person, who's a challenge in your small group? Why is that person's behavior a challenge to you? What might your partner(s) suggest as a way to deal with that challenge?
- What's something you've learned about facilitating a group you wish you would have known earlier?
- On a scale of one to ten, how's the trust level in your group? In what ways does that reflect how trusting you are—or aren't—of other people?
- When it comes to encouragement, who are you encouraging in your group? Who is someone—in your group or not—who's encouraging you in your walk with Jesus?
- Which tip in Chapter 23 do you want to make absolutely sure you don't forget to plug into your small group leadership toolbox?

CHAPTER 21

RECOMMENDED LEADERSHIP RESOURCES

Countdown: Launching and Leading Transformational Groups, David Francis and Rick Howerton, LifeWay Press (2014)

A Different Kind of Tribe: Embracing the New Small-Group Dynamic, Rick Howerton, NavPress (2012)

Why Didn't You Warn Me: How to Deal With Challenging Group Members, Pat J. Sikora, Standard Publishing (2007)
Available at mightyoakministries.com

Leading Small Groups That Thrive, Ryan T Hartwig, Courtney W Davis, Jason A Sniff, Zondervan (2020)

Small Groups with Purpose: How to Create Healthy Communities, Steve Gladen, Baker Books (2011)

If you provide childcare and want flexible, multi-age, low-supply lessons designed for in-home use, check out these books:
13 Very Bad Days and How God Fixed Them; 13 Amazing Animals and How God Used Them; 13 Very Cool Stories and Why Jesus Told Them, Mikal Keefer, David C Cook (various release dates)

ABOUT THE CONTRIBUTORS

*O*ne thing the generous people who contributed to this book have in common: They're all in a small group...just not the same one. So we tracked them down, asked for their insights, and they were kind enough to share.

Rick Howerton has served as a collegiate pastor, small group pastor, teaching pastor, church planter, and all-around small groups guy. He's an author of books, studies, and small group leader training resources, and currently serves the Baptist Convention as Church Consultant for the South-Central Region of Kentucky. His goal is to see "a biblical small group within walking distance of every person on the planet."

Michael Fleming is the creator of 2ndmanunited.com and, since his 20's, has explored how to narrow the gap between Christian belief and Christian behavior in his church and community. Check out his blogs at 2ndmanunited.com for insights into what makes for a healthy church and healthy small groups.

Carter Moss is a programmer turned Campus Pastor serving Newbreak Church in San Diego, California. He's also an Editorial Advisor at SmallGroups.com, has dreams of being a volleyball powerhouse, and has more Facebook friends that should be humanly possible.

Pat J. Sikora is a popular author and conference speaker. She's also founder of Mighty Oak Ministries and has been involved with small group ministries for more than 40 years.

Reid Smith is the Director of Communities of Purpose for the Small Group Network and has served as Pastor of Groups at Christ Fellowship Church in Palm Beach County, Florida. He's passionate about encouraging small group leaders—like you.

John Cutshall is a minister, certified Christian Leadership Coach, radio personality, author, and former Bible college dean. He's currently living in Indiana but has a habit of showing up where you don't expect him.

Thanks to these small group leaders whose insights shaped this book: Brad, Nick, Donna, Susan, Carlos, Mike, and Cherie. (*Due to the personal nature of their stories, some names of people in this list have been changed to ensure confidentiality.*)

Writer
Mikal Keefer is a Christian writer who has published more than 35 books for children, youth, and adults, as well as writing for a wide array of magazines and curricula. He's been part of small groups for decades as a leader, group member, trainer, and cookie-bringer.

General Editor
Matt Lockhart spent more than twenty-five years serving in a variety of editorial and leadership roles in Christian publishing at Serendipity House, Group, and Standard/David C Cook. With a penchant for product development, he continues to enjoy helping to create Kingdom focused resources like the *Outreach Ministry Guides*. And though he's the General Editor, you aren't required to address him as "General" when you next see him.

SMALL GROUP TEAM CONTACT INFORMATION

Names   Phone and Email

_____   _____

_____   _____

_____   _____

_____   _____

_____   _____

_____   _____

_____   _____

_____   _____

_____   _____

SMALL GROUP TEAM NOTES

SMALL GROUP TEAM NOTES

SMALL GROUP TEAM NOTES

How Can a Prayer Ministry Transform Your Church?

Whether you are part of your church's prayer ministry, or thinking about starting or joining a prayer ministry team, the *Prayer Ministry Volunteer Handbook* is for you!

We are often very quick to say we will pray for someone when we hear they are going through tough times, but do we actually follow through with our promise to pray for them? How many times do we turn to prayer only in times of crisis, as a last resort, or simply to ask things of God?

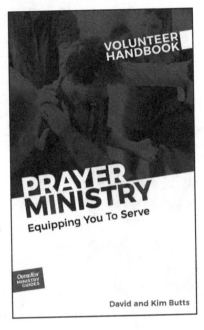

We need to make prayer the first course of action, guiding all of our life decisions. We must challenge ourselves to move beyond the dinnertime and bedtime prayers and progress to a thoughtful conversation with Christ.

Join authors David and Kim Butts as they explore how a well-equipped church prayer ministry team can serve as a model and an encouragement to support the members of the congregation, and even the pastoral staff, in their prayer journeys. Discover how you can make your church a house of prayer for all believers.

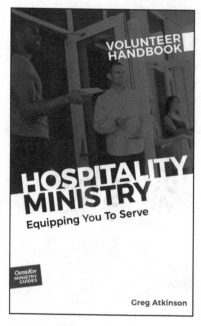

Be Our Guest

Whether you are a volunteer in your church's guest services ministry, or thinking about serving alongside ushers, greeters, welcome desk hosts, and parking lot attendants at your church, the *Hospitality Ministry Volunteer Handbook* is for you!

How does a member of community see your church? When they hear your church's name, what is their initial reaction? We want any individual who steps foot onto our church campus to immediately feel Christ's love through our actions toward them—the question is, are we doing a good job at accomplishing that mission?

We might not think of customer service and church hospitality in the same vein, but this book shows how a service mentality can make life-changing first impressions on newcomers. It's filled with specific, practical strategies and tools to help the hospitality ministry team show the love of Christ to every visitor.

Join author Greg Atkinson as he helps identify ways your church can increase its hospitality to the community around you, and, ultimately, reach those people for the Kingdom of God.

Practical Outreach Ideas and Ministry Tools

Never has there been a greater need to share the good news of God's love with those in our communities. This compact handbook shows how individual Christians and ministry teams can share the gospel by reaching out to and serving others.

Featuring 121 outreach ideas, this book helps to equip ministry teams with practical tools to serve families, children, youth, seniors, first responders, the oppressed and under resourced, millennials, single parents, local schools and businesses and more!

Designed for ministry volunteers, the book is a compact handbook of outreach ministry helps, which in addition to the dozens of outreach ideas also include outreach Scriptures and prayers, ways to share your faith, team discussion questions and recommended outreach ministries and resources.

This helpful little book is a great resource for equipping outreach ministry volunteers to serve others and to share the good news!

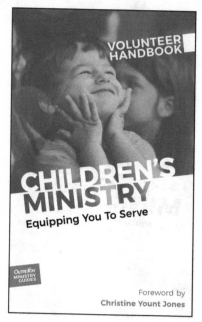

VOLUNTEER HANDBOOK

CHILDREN'S MINISTRY

Equipping You To Serve

Foreword by
Christine Yount Jones

Equipping Children's Ministry Volunteers

Whether you are part of your church's children's ministry, or thinking about serving in children's ministry, the *Children's Ministry Volunteer Handbook* is for you!

Too often, people view children's ministry as a place to drop off the kids so the adults can listen to the sermon, uninterrupted. They fail to see the power and potential of children's ministry.

In Matthew 19:13-14, Jesus said, "Let the little children come to me, and do not hinder them, for the kingdom of heaven belongs to such as these." While we may see the naivete of children as a detriment, Jesus sees it as a strength—there is beauty in the simplicity of the gospel. Investing in children's ministry is a worthwhile and crucial part of the church.

This practical handbook features insights from six authors, all experts in the field of children's ministry, with over 100 years of combined experience. They will help guide you through the challenges and joys of children's ministry—and how it is vital to the Kingdom of God.

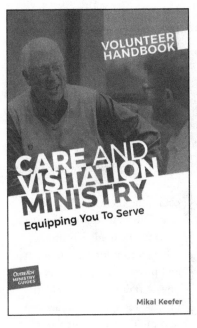

VOLUNTEER HANDBOOK

CARE AND VISITATION MINISTRY

Equipping You To Serve

OUTREACH MINISTRY GUIDES

Mikal Keefer

Talk About More Than the Weather

You've driven to the hospital and stand outside a patient's room, ready to knock and ask permission to enter. But then what? How do you make a visit that actually matters?

Here are hundreds of practical tips gleaned from the experience of veteran visitors—chaplains, pastors, and volunteers who've made thousands of visits in hospitals, nursing care facilities, rehab centers, homes, hospice centers, even prisons.

They share what to do, what not to do, and how to connect in caring, compassionate ways with people who may be experiencing the worst days of their lives.

Discover how to make visits that matter—that literally change lives—as you carry the love of Jesus to those who are sick, lonely, or simply curious about the Kingdom.

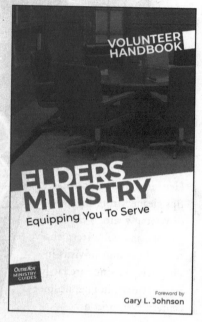

Biblical Guidance and Practical Advice for Church Elders and Perspective Elders

Equip church elders to lead well. More than better methods, the church today needs better leaders. But too often we recruit these leaders (the New Testament calls them *elders*) without equipping them for their vital task. This practical handbook presents the need, lifts up the Bible's vision for elder ministry, and provides a wealth of practical how-to training to help elders provide the spiritual leadership that can't come from anyone else. Elder teams will build unity and confidence as they discuss it together.

Written by the ministry founders and leaders of e2: effective elders, content is based on decades of local-church experience and interaction with everyday elders in hundreds of congregations.